Money Issues
for Christians Today

Money Issues
for Christians Today

by

David L. Martin

Rod and Staff Publishers, Inc.
P.O. Box 3, Hwy. 172
Crockett, Kentucky 41413-0003
Telephone: (606) 522-4348

Printed in U. S. A.

ISBN 978-07399-2406-8

Catalog no. 2268

3   4   5   6   7   —   27   26   25   24   23   22   21   20   19   18

Table of Contents

Introduction

Over the years, authors have written many books about money. Yet new books on money keep coming. Why did the writer of this book go to the trouble? Why not simply refer you to books that have already been written? What does this book offer that other books do not?

Well, every book is unique and meets the needs of unique individuals. If not everyone benefits from this book, others will find in it just the word they need. An old encyclopedia makes this comment about John Greenleaf Whittier: "Whittier's poetry is not considered great, but it is simple and sincere and has always appealed to the people for whom he wrote." If someone says that about this book, that is all that matters.

Besides, most books on money do not hold high the principles taught in the Bible. They say some sensible things, but their sense is based on a foundation of unreliable suppositions. It is a bit rash to say, "This time around, we are going to say everything right." But we will try, and we will use the Bible for our base.

If you find anything in this imperfect book that is indigestible to you, please lay the matter aside for now and read on. This book was meant to be food for thought, not for frustration.

Front cover photograph used by permission from Appalachian Point of View.

"But this I say, brethren, the time is short: it remaineth, that both they that have wives be as though they had none; and they that weep, as though they wept not; and they that rejoice, as though they rejoiced not; and they that buy, as though they possessed not . . . for the fashion of this world passeth away."

1 Corinthians 7:29–31

1. Planning

Setting Priorities

Life is a journey.

Some time ago, a family from the West planned a trip east. They knew they wanted to finally arrive at Grandpa's place; that was easy. It took a little more planning to figure out where to stop along the way. They settled upon stopping with friends in Utah, with other friends in Nebraska, and at a motel in Indiana. The Lord foiled their motel plans in Indiana, though, by letting Father lose his wallet long enough for them to seek shelter with friends—only to let him find it again as soon as they arrived at their friends' house! They saved considerable money that night and renewed an old friendship.

Finally they arrived at Grandpa's place, having eaten supper along the way—only to discover that supper was waiting for them! Obviously, they made some mistakes along the way; but just as obviously, they arrived safe and sound—and happy too—because their general direction was right.

Once again, life is a journey. We need to determine where we finally want to arrive, which is in eternal glory with God Himself. To most people, that is easy and obvious.

To be sensible, however, we ought to plan where we hope to be at certain points along the way. That is where most people fail. They do not want to think about what God expects them to be doing today, tomorrow, next week, and next year. The old-fashioned

> *"Prepare in summer for winter, in youth for old age, and in time for eternity."*[1]

word for this kind of failure is *disobedience.* It will finally take people to an eternal destiny they do not want.

Christians make plans. This does not mean that our plans are always perfect. Just as the Lord alters people's travel plans, He sometimes alters our plans in the journey of life. However, we should make plans. (For how can the Lord change them if we do not make any?)

Although we are thinking now of financial goals rather than spiritual ones, we cannot altogether divorce the two. Our financial steps along the way will help or hinder us on our way toward heaven.

Many people are short-term planners. They live for the present. Future plans surrender to little present emergencies because "a bird in the hand is worth two in the bush." They do not save for a future house, because they want a late-model car now. They do not save for doctor bills, because it is too much fun to spend money now on the kinds of things that make doctor bills later.

Such people are not as happy as they seem.

Did you ever hear of the marshmallow test? A researcher would say to a young child, "Here's a marshmallow for you to eat while I'm gone for a few minutes. But if you wait to eat it until I come back, I will give you another marshmallow. Then you will have two." Predictably, the children reacted differently. Some ate their marshmallows right away; others saved them.

Researchers kept track of those children in the years that followed. The children who could save their marshmallows grew up to enjoy more happiness and success than the ones who did not. That too was predictable. Anyone who has read the story of Esau selling his birthright for a bowl of soup could guess that he would marry wrong too.

Some people do plan for the future. If they want to vacation in Arizona next summer, they sacrifice the pleasure of dining at the Family Restaurant tonight. Or they may sacrifice the vacation in Arizona because they want a comfortable retirement. They plan ten years ahead, then twenty . . . forty . . . sixty.

But here is the curious thing—they stop! If they can plan ahead far enough for retirement, why can they not plan ahead just twenty years more? Some time ago a leading magazine came out with the statement, "A sound financial plan can make your retirement years truly golden."[2] Very well, but what about the years, or rather the ages, beyond retirement?

If there is one sin that damns more souls than any other, it is probably mental laziness—the unwillingness to make tough decisions. A few people do lose their souls by deliberately choosing to do wrong. But most people who lose their souls do so by merely neglecting to do right. People generally do not plan to fail; they just fail to plan. The bigger the decision, the bigger the temptation to put it off.

> *"He who provides for this life but takes no care for eternity is wise for a moment but a fool forever."[3]*

Since life is a journey, why do people fail to plan for it? Besides succumbing to mental laziness, people fall victim to the feeling that the way things are is the way things will always be. During winter, it feels as if winter will always be. During summer, we think it will never again cool off. When we are children, we think childhood will never end. And when we live on planet Earth, it feels as if this is the only kind of existence there ever was or ever will be. "All things continue as they were" is the general feeling.

Do not be fooled. The journey of life has an end, a date on the calendar already known to God. If we want that date to be a happy one, we must make some wise decisions along the way.

Thankfully, God takes a keen interest in the outcome of our journey. If we as His children keep looking His way for His directions, we need not worry.

Why Keep Records?

Good financial management starts with keeping records. If you do not know which direction you have come from, how can you tell which direction to go? Looking back over the past year, you can see where your money has come from and where it has gone. The best historians turn out to be the best prophets.

Since the advent of income tax, people have been compelled to keep financial records of their income. So it is assumed that you know where your money came from. But perhaps you do not know where your money went. The least you could do to prevent this from happening in the future is to keep your receipts. Then even if you do not have a detailed record of all your expenses, you will have something to fall back on if you have questions.

How should you keep receipts? There must be many ways, but here is a very simple one for a start. On an ordinary business envelope, write the name of the present month (*January,* for example) and the word *Expenses.* On another (since you might as well keep track of your income in the same way), write the name of the month and the word *Income.* Whenever you buy something, put the receipt into the Expenses envelope. Whenever you receive any income, put whatever record you have of it into the Income envelope.

You can easily expand this system whenever you like. If you want to keep track of expenses in one category, such as vehicle expenses, you might want to keep an envelope in your car. Put your gas receipts inside this envelope, and scribble your mileage records on the outside.

Where should you store your envelopes? One man is pleased with his top right-hand desk drawer, which he has divided with homemade cardboard partitions into twelve compartments, one for each month. That is a good place, not only for your receipt and expense envelopes but also for bills, bank statements, and the like. For long-term storage, you can use the time-honored shoeboxes, with rubber bands around each month's envelopes.

If you prefer, you can store all your records by subject. One person's expandable record file has pockets labeled "Automobile," "Bank Account," "Bills," "Correspondence," "Dental/Medical," "Education," and so on. The pocket labeled "Receipts" is jammed. A number of other pockets contain nothing at all. This is one reason for preferring the month-by-month system. It is neater because each month has approximately the same number of papers. And you do not have to look very long for various phone bills, even if they are in different pockets of your system.

If you have never kept track of your expenses before, you have a few surprises coming. A young person probably spends less on clothes than he might have expected, but much more on his car. That is one good reason to postpone getting a car as long as possible.

> *"A fool and his money are soon parted."*[4]

You might also be surprised at how much money gets away in small expenditures. Something that costs you only ten dollars a week will cost *five hundred twenty dollars* in a year. Seeing where the money is leaking away will definitely affect your planning.

14

Budgeting Your Money

A budget is an organized plan for spending your money. Just how detailed should it be?

Some people keep track of every penny they spend. They seem to love keeping records. But other people hate it. That probably means they should keep records for sure. Yet if they keep track of the most basic things like savings and church offerings, making sure they have enough money for those, they might make out well by just letting other things fall into place. It is better to follow a simple budget than to set up an elaborate one only to get frustrated with it in the end.

The number one thing you should budget is your thank offering to the Lord. Guesstimating does not work. Someone who simply puts into the offering whatever he thinks he can afford, waiting to tally the results till the end of the year, will probably

The envelope system. Some families have found that the best way for them to budget is to close down their checking account and deal strictly in cash. (A compromise would be to use the checking account only for certain items like utility bills and house payments.) When they get any money, they divide it among envelopes marked (for instance) "Groceries," "Rent," "Car," "Miscellaneous," "Medical," "Church offering," and "Savings."

Then everything about their finances is plain and obvious. Either they have money for groceries, or they do not. Either they have money for rent—well, rent is a fixed expense, so the rent envelope gets filled first and goes strictly for rent. Let's try again. Either they have enough money for the phone bill in the "Phone" envelope, or (if that bill is a little higher than what they expected) they take the money out of an envelope marked "Oops," which they keep for the times when a certain account runs short.

You might wonder how people who deal strictly in cash pay bills that are marked, "Do not send cash." One way other than keeping a checking account is to use money orders. These are available not only at banks but also at post offices. "And at some grocery stores," said a lady at the bank when she was asked. Then she added in a whisper, "They're probably cheaper too!"

Since even the cheaper money orders are more expensive than checks, you should figure what each system will cost per month before opting for the advantages of not using checks.

15

discover at the end of the year that he is a thousand dollars in debt to the Lord. Better make a new resolution! When money comes, with all due speed set aside the Lord's share to put in the offering. (Let us assume a tenth.) It will relieve you to know that you are keeping up to date, and you will be surprised to discover that your new system does not put you in the hole.

A tenth of what? Not a tenth of all the money that flows through your hands if you are a farmer or a businessman. In other words, do not calculate on the gross income. If you did that, you might have nothing left to live on and might be in debt to the Lord besides.

Rather, calculate on the basis of what is left after your business expenses are paid. (Not that you pay off all your business debts before you give. But do subtract this month's payment before you calculate the tenth.) What you pay a tenth on will be roughly the same as the adjusted gross income (AGI) on your income tax return. This is your income before income taxes, not afterward. You would give a tenth of the amount you have before deducting the grocery bill, right? Well, giving before deducting income taxes is no different. And if you have received a considerable amount in gifts, you will want to give a tenth of that too, even if it is not taxable.

After you have given the Lord His share, what is next? Another tenth should go into savings. If you can do this on your before-tax income, so much the better. If you calculate on the amount after tax, you will save less, but even then a tenth is a respectable amount. Have a system; that is the main thing.

You say you cannot afford to save a thing? Maybe you can't, depending on where you are in life. However, if you are young and single and you have a job that pays well, you should be able to save quite a bit more than a tenth. Even people who find saving difficult may discover that it is easier than it looks, once they do it systematically.

All right, offering first and then savings. What next?

The bills. There is something about bills that you cannot gainsay. They will sit there until you write out the checks. That is just as well, since you have to pay them anyway.

If you are young and on your own, maybe the only bill you have to pay is room and board to your parents. If you are a homeowner, you need no introduction to bills for electricity, telephone, and heating fuel. Maybe you are also paying off a mortgage. Maybe you have medical bills.

Notice that I did not mention credit card bills here. Credit cards in themselves actually cost little (depending on the card). They are a temporary convenience, but they do not make the bills larger or smaller. Resist the

> *If you are a wage earner, the government does some budgeting for you by taking income tax off your pay. Just because it is done for you does not mean you should not pay attention. Perhaps you can reduce your income tax by using approved methods. See "The tax benefits of living savingly," pages 79 and 80.*

temptation to charge a number of things and then lump them together under "credit card." That is much too vague and prevents intelligent planning.

And after the bills? Household expenses, such as food and clothing. Vehicle expenses, such as gas, oil, and repairs.

And leave some room in your budget for miscalculations and other small emergencies. The electric or phone bill may be unusually high this month. There will be the broken tooth, the ruined tire, the balky furnace. These are what might be called "normal emergencies." If we gasp in shock every time we need a repair or must go to the doctor, we are not being realistic. A flat tire is not necessarily a chastening from God or a messenger of Satan—it is probably just a flat tire.

What about the large emergencies? Some of them you have no control over and will simply have to pick up the pieces afterward with help from your savings and from other Christians. But some things you can plan and save for ahead of time. You should know whether or not your car will last much longer, and whether a baby will soon arrive in your household. Normally you will be able to save up money for these things.

Also remember the simple but significant words "cash flow." It is not enough to have a total annual income high enough to cover the total expenses for the year. You must have the money when you need it. If you know that your flow of income will slow in the summer or the winter, you will naturally want to get your biggest expenses out of the way during the season when you have the most money.

The cash-flow concept is fraught with frustrations. Suppose you want to build a shop or close in the back porch of your house. Someone has observed: "When you have the money, you don't have the time; and when you have the time, you don't have the money." There are no easy answers to this dilemma, but at least you know that you have sympathy.

A budget will vary quite a bit with people. A mail carrier using his own car has an expense that never occurs to the rest of us—he has to service his brakes several times a year. The expense involved in this should not take him by surprise.

Budgeting will vary at different stages of life. A young person with a good, steady job should be able to live on a fraction of his income. Middle-aged people with half-grown children might consume everything they produce, and wish for more. Old people, of course, will usually consume more than they produce. But we treasure them for reasons other than their economic value.

The Value of Limited Finances

Some years ago an elderly gentleman needed two surgeries at once—one to improve circulation to his head and another to improve circulation to his leg. What do you think the doctor did?

The doctor told him, "We will do surgery on the blood vessels in your neck first. You can live without your leg, but you can't live without your head."

Like that doctor, we must frankly admit that we cannot do everything at once, that our resources are limited. True, we can draw on all of heaven's resources, as many of us are much too slow to learn. But God wants us to learn more lessons than just that. He wants us to live with limits for the time being.

A Christian brother told of walking into a religious bookstore and meeting a lively salesman who wanted to sell him books. "Here's a book you should have! And here's another one I think should be on your shelf!"

"I can't afford all those books just now," the brother said.

"Your Father is rich, isn't he?" the salesman asked.

The brother responded, "Yes! My Father is very rich! Bring

on the books, and charge them to my Father!"

The brother concluded with a smile, "I don't think he brought a single book."

Why does God keep us limited financially?

Well, we are like the servants in Jesus' story of the talents. The master gave his servants five talents, or two, or one, "to every man according to his several ability" (Matthew 25:15). Any sensible employer knows he can give more responsibility to some employees than to others—this said with all due respect to the less capable employees. However, no employee has unlimited ability. And any employee can be overloaded.

God's limits on us are actually His mercy to us, "for unto whomsoever much is given, of him shall be much required" (Luke 12:48). Sometimes for purposes of His own, God does let individuals get very rich. Some of them take the opportunity to do good, but more often they largely miss, or mismanage, that opportunity. Someday they will need to answer for their record, as we all must do. Most of us are better off with less opportunity to bring spiritual calamity on ourselves.

Then too, we need each other, and our personal limits remind us of that. If we had too much money, we would become too independent. Arguably, we have too much money already in North America, judging from the general loss of community spirit.

> *Andrew Carnegie is supposed to have said, "Millionaires seldom smile."*[5]

And we need the Lord. That fact also becomes pretty foggy in our minds when we can simply go to the bank to make all our wants and wishes known.

Curiously, even Christ lived with limits when He was here on earth. Think of it—Jesus went through practically all of His life at walking speed. Once in a while, He traveled in a slow sailboat. He had little or no money. In some ways He was much more limited than we are. Yet at the close of His life, He prayed, "I have glorified thee on the earth: I have finished the work which thou gavest me to do" (John 17:4).

Why did even Jesus have to live within limits? Here is one reason: it helped Him to identify with the people He was trying to help. He "was in all points tempted like as we are" (Hebrews 4:15).

19

"For in that he himself hath suffered being tempted, he is able to succour them that are tempted" (Hebrews 2:18). If Jesus could do it, we can too. By accepting our limits, we will gain more than we lose. Our limits will help us to identify with others, and they will feel a comradeship with us.

Remember that it takes stress to make things grow. Maybe we could compare our financial restrictions to gravity. Gravity restricts us, sometimes uncomfortably, but without it our bones and muscles would deteriorate—to say nothing about the problem of keeping our feet on the ground. We are stronger with gravity than without it.

By the same token, without financial restrictions and challenges, we would always be weak. We would never grow properly. We would always be children. But with restrictions, we can more easily "grow up into him in all things, which is the head, even Christ" (Ephesians 4:15).

Zero

In the old days, either you had money or you did not. If you had money, you could buy things. If you didn't have money, you couldn't. A zero was a zero.

Things are not as simple these days. It is easy to buy on credit and pay a bill at the end of the month. And then it is but another step to get overdraft protection at the bank so you can overdraw your checking account with impunity. Going into outright debt is yet another step. What happened to zero?

It is still there. Even people who do not mind going into debt will finally come to the end of the end. That is their zero.

A man we will call James found that out the hard way. He was facing a high income tax bill and was wondering how to pay it.

"If you are in a hole, stop digging."

So he went to the bank and arranged for $2,000 in overdraft protection. That was nice at first. He had deeper pockets now. He could write a check for $200, even if he had only $100 in the bank, and not get slapped for it (except for interest).

But finally he bumped against the bottom of the overdraft protection. Then he began to understand. He had not gotten rid of that pesky zero. He had only shifted it. Now he was at zero again; only it was two thousand dollars below ground level!

After bumping along for a while at that level, James found a way to pay off the overdrawn amount. He also told the bank to cancel the setup. Sometime later, he hit bottom again, but at ground level this time. He had nothing to

> *"You know," said a woman to a friend in financial trouble, "if we don't have the money for something, we don't get it."*
> *Her friend looked blank. "How does that work?"*

fall back on anymore—no savings, nothing of his own. But this time he chose to bump along on *top* of the ground.

"Aha!" says some reader. "The zero is movable. Why not climb a ladder and peg the zero two thousand dollars *up* instead of down?"

That is actually not a bad point. If you can shift your zero downward to your detriment, why not shift your zero upward to your advantage? The government already does that. From your paycheck, the government takes tax money that you never even see. You spend on the basis of the money you have left—take-home pay, we call it. Your zero has been shifted.

Take ten percent off to give to the Lord. That money was never yours in the first place, so spend on the basis of what you have left. Shift your zero.

The zero concept applies not only to what you spend but also to what you have already invested. Think of a person who owns a house. He has trouble paying his bills. Should he sell the house

Friend's comment: A literal way to reset the zero upward is to keep an invisible "reserve" amount in your checking account. We started doing that years ago when we opened a checking account that required a $100 minimum balance. The bank charges a $5 fee if the balance goes below $100. So we put, say, $500 into the account but entered only $400 as our beginning balance. Each month when we reconcile the account, we just remember that our balance is $100 lower than the bank's. In fact, we've increased the reserve to $200 so we have an extra $100 that we can use if things run a little tight. But in many months, we never go into the reserve.

in order to pay them? After all, if he has money in the house, he has money. So he is well above zero!

Maybe he should sell—but probably not. Our zero need not always be at the point of destitution. It can be at a point somewhere above that.

A family told of a time when they were down to the point where they had nothing. They had money in a property, but they did not think it was right to touch that. They placed the zero above it.

Things got very tight. They were down to fifty cents or so. One day, one of the daughters, feeling grouchy because of all their problems, went to the mailbox. In the snow she saw an envelope that had come in the mail before but had been accidentally dropped. In the envelope was enough money to tide them over.

Why is it that if we hang at zero long enough, we find a way through? Perhaps it is partly because we discover ways to sacrifice and save and maybe even earn, that we did not think of before. Perhaps it is also because when we come to the point of desperation, we look up to the Lord in a way we never did before,

Writer's question to friend: What about running your checking account into the hole, figuring that the checks you have mailed out haven't all been cashed yet; and by the time they are, you'll have more money in the bank? Is this permissible in a pinch?

Answer: As you might know, such a check is called a kite and the practice is called kiting. I consider it acceptable in a pinch, but only if I'm quite sure that the deposit will be in the bank in good time, and if I have a backup in case something goes wrong. In fact, I'm thinking of using that method this month. A payment to a bank in Richmond, Va., is due on Jan. 24, and my next direct deposit from my employer is scheduled to be in on Jan. 22. I plan to mail the payment on Jan. 20 and call my bank on Jan. 22 to verify that the deposit has come in. If it hasn't, I can make a transfer from another account to cover the check.

To illustrate how things can go wrong: I once mailed a check to a local bank on Monday and started writing checks on the deposit right away. About Thursday they called and said my account was overdrawn. I told them about mailing the deposit, and they said (I think) that they would wait and see if it comes in. It finally arrived on Friday, three days late! The bank was nice enough to cancel the overdraft charges, but it was a nerve-racking situation—and a learning experience.

and we experience answers to prayers that He was waiting for us to pray.

George Müller once wrote, "I was determined to wait upon God only, and not to work an unscriptural deliverance for myself. I have thousands of pounds set aside for the building fund, but I would not touch it. . . . When I was first converted, I would have said, 'What harm can there be to use some of the money which has been given for the building fund? God will help me eventually with money for the orphans, and then I can replace it.' But each time we work a deliverance of our own, we find it more difficult to trust in God. At last we give way entirely to our natural reasoning, and unbelief prevails."[6]

Does this mean we can place a zero anywhere we please? No. If we could, we would keep thinking of more and more things we supposedly cannot do without, go out and buy them, and then expect God to help us pay our other bills before our checkbook balance drops below zero. That would not be good for us, since we need the discipline of doing without. We also need the humbling experience of praying "Give us this day our daily bread" and wondering how the Lord will provide it.

If we are within the Lord's will to hold certain possessions, then certainly He will make a way for us to hold and use them, not only for our own satisfaction but also for His.

Too Much Money
at the End of the Month

Once you have spent for your needs, money left over is quite a pleasant predicament! You feel like a child in a candy store. A dozen delights clamor for your attention. The money is yours, so why not get what you want?

> *"For unto whomsoever much is given, of him shall be much required"* (Luke 12:48).

Why not? Remember when you were a child? You saw a toy on the store shelf and wanted it ever so badly. If you had just this one wish, you would never ask for another toy! By now you know it does not work that way.

A few extra pleasures might have been all right. But finally, your parents kept a tight rein on your wants, didn't they? It built your character to do without some things. Now it is your turn to be your own parent.

But just what should you do with your extra money? You might give more to the Lord, put more in savings, or both. You might invest in livestock if you have the interest and the space. You might help to buy braces for some child's teeth (with parental knowledge and consent, of course). You might buy a good microscope, complete with slides and cover slips, for the school. There are all kinds of interesting possibilities.

Maybe instead of thinking in terms of money, you should think in terms of time. Since you have money, you can afford to take a day off now and then to help someone, providing you do not inconvenience your employer. If you are a man, you can help pour concrete for someone's basement, or help take down a neighbor's old dead tree, or milk cows for the farmer with a sprained ankle. If you are a woman, you can baby-sit for the sister who has to run to the doctor, or write a story for a children's periodical, or bake extra buns for someone who loves them but does not have time to make them.

Too Much Month
at the End of the Money

The other dilemma is not so pleasant. What if the budget does not hold out?

It is easy for a writer to sit in a swivel chair and advise other people what to do. But finally it is a choice between two. You have to stay within your budget, or else you have to spend beyond the limits of your income. I am not talking about overspending your income if you know you can make it up next fall. I am talking about overspending without any idea of how you will make it up.

Now you expect me to say, "Never overspend like that." But I will not say it. There are times when the income is barely sufficient or not sufficient at all. Those times can be distressingly frequent when you have growing children, whose appetites are good and whose shoes are constantly wearing out.

The ways of cutting expenses that you come up with might not work. You might say, "Well, we can live on beans and potatoes." Sorry, some people cannot do that without getting sick. Besides, maybe the schoolteacher is boarding with you, and you can't feed her like that when you are getting paid to keep her!

If things are not holding out, ask yourself if you have done something wrong. Maybe you have not. On the other hand, maybe you have, and the Lord wants you to recognize it.

Is your giving up to date? If not, is it because you have never set up a system of giving? Or perhaps you have a system but have fallen behind.

Do you have a spiritual problem in some other area of life? Not that you should assume whenever God withholds His blessing that you must have done something wrong. Job's friends made that assumption, to their own embarrassment. One can too easily assume something is wrong with a person spiritually just because he is poor. Still, it is a possibility worth asking yourself about.

Are you giving *too much?* A strange question indeed, and one that calls for an explanation!

The Bible teaches that different people have different gifts.

For example, Romans 12 says, "Having then gifts differing according to the grace that is given to us." The passage mentions prophesying, ministering, teaching, and exhorting, and then it says, "He that giveth, let him do it with simplicity." So giving is one of the gifts. It is a privilege to be able to give, and God expects everyone to do some giving. Some people have more of the gift; some have less.

But if your major gift is teaching, preaching, and writing, you probably do not have the gift of giving much beyond your standard tenth. Must you also take on the major burdens of church finances? Must you be everyone's rich uncle?

Even in such a case, there might be nothing wrong with your lending money to a Christian friend or organization at a reasonable interest rate. But interest-free loans and outright grants are another matter. There are people in the church who can shoulder that kind of thing. You might—or might not—be one of them.

True, the widow gave her last mite, and maybe you should too. But here we are simply pointing out the other side—that maybe you should not.

If you have a known purpose in mind, it is a mistake for you to give all your resources away and then expect things to be handed to you. If you want to buy a car, normally you should save up for it. If you want to buy a house, do likewise.

To be fair, no doubt there are people who have wondered if they gave too much in their youth. But now they have friends coming up with all kinds of excuses to help them out (even supplying them with vehicles or housing). You do not have to hit the exact level of giving exactly right. If you must err, err on the side of generosity. The Lord knows your heart, and He takes care of His own.

In summary, if your budget does not hold out, it may not mean something is wrong between you and the Lord. Perhaps He wants you to see your resources dwindle so you depend more on Him. Or maybe He is urging you to do practical, mature things that give you a measure of independence from other people. You can learn as much about the Christian life from disciplining yourself to earn a living and to manage money as you can from experiencing poverty.

Budgeting Your Time

As any poor man knows, the first rule of money management is . . .

Have money.

Budgeting money, therefore, must begin with budgeting your time because time is what you need to earn money. In fact, Benjamin Franklin said, "Time is money." That is an oversimplification, no doubt, but there is a connection.

I suggest that you budget your time only to the extent that you feel comfortable. If you want to sit down and block out your day the way a teacher fills out a plan book, fine. On the other hand, if you prefer a simple first-things-first approach and can keep your system in your head, that is fine too.

Of course, you cannot always just do as you please. Sometimes you must endure the discomfort of managing your time by a specific plan, like it or not. It will save frustration in the end. Suppose you start out a day by seeing something to do and doing it; then you see something else to do and you do that; and on you go, doing any job that catches your attention at the moment. In the evening you will realize that there were certain things you *really* wanted to do that you failed to get done. That is the price of not managing your time.

Most people find that much time budgeting is done for them. They have a full-time job, and the boss tells them what time to start work in the morning and what time to go home in the evening. That is good. Some people who have tried working at home finally gave it up with a sigh and returned to a regular job. They loved being at home, but they could not keep their noses to the grindstone.

Even working full-time still leaves us with some time to manage on evenings and weekends. So then all of us, whether working by our own schedule or someone else's, can benefit from the principles given below.

Budget your earliest moments. The Hebrews were sensible folks; they began their day at sundown. So much about the success of a day depends on how well we managed the previous evening and what time we got ourselves to bed. If today is going wrong,

> "Prepare thy work without,
> and make it fit for
> thyself in the field; and
> afterwards build thine house"
> (Proverbs 24:27).

it might be last evening's fault. If we learn our lesson and manage this evening right, tomorrow will probably go much better. This rule applies especially to teachers and students, who obviously must do some preparing for the next day, but it is not limited to them.

By the way, besides starting each day early enough, start each week early enough. A fool and his Monday are soon parted.

Do prime things during prime time. In other words, if something seems so urgent that you must stop your work to do it, ask yourself if you can put it off until the evening or Saturday.

Take mowing the lawn, for instance. That is something important and good to do. But if you spend most of Tuesday morning to do the mowing, will you be able to make up your lost earnings after supper?

Recently I read of an elderly man who wished he still had the strength and energy to work full days. He needs the money. But his neighbors remember times when he was shooting groundhogs and planting potatoes instead of doing more gainful work. Certainly, planting potatoes is work, but there are times when other things come ahead of it.

The same might be true of reading to a child. If your three-year-old comes at ten in the morning and says, "I want someone to read to me," it is perfectly acceptable to explain that you do not read books now, because this is working time. (We are thinking of fathers now, not necessarily mothers or hired girls.) Children should learn that there is a time and a place for everything.

A helpful rule might be that you will not interrupt your work at home for something unless you would interrupt your "work at work" for that. Of course, there

> To insist on being left alone
> to work does have snares. Children
> understand why you would not come
> home from work to settle a squabble
> on the living-room floor, but they
> will not understand why you do not
> come out of your study.

are times when you *would* interrupt your work at work, so it is right to interrupt your work at home on those occasions.

Then too, you need break times. But even break times can multiply like rabbits if you are not careful. One family setting up a business learned that it was best for them to take scheduled breaks and do their talking during those breaks. If they did their talking at odd moments throughout the day, they often ended up taking too much time away from their work.

Keep up your momentum. If you have a project going and a day comes when you hardly have time for it, try not to skip it entirely. Give it a few minutes at least. Otherwise, you are in danger of losing your momentum and having a hard time getting started again in the future—if you ever get restarted at all. Giving it a token effort helps to keep that slot in your schedule.

Sometimes a seeming break in the momentum actually helps to produce momentum. One minister, needing to prepare a sermon on Saturday, sometimes likes to spend a half hour on it, then half an hour on something else, then a half hour on the sermon, and so on.

The reason for this? A big block of time gives too much opportunity to get bogged down and to lose momentum. But a half hour comes to a sudden end after thirty minutes, keeping him awake and reminding him that his time is limited. It gives a marching rhythm to his day.

A writer who has lost his writing momentum may want to keep one eye on the clock and then record the time every five minutes on his manuscript or computer screen. This helps him be aware as to whether or not he is getting things done. And it gives him a prodding every five minutes.

Take time for downtime. When you are lying down to sleep, it does not feel as if you are getting anything done. Is sleep therefore a waste of time? No; rather, sleepiness is a waste of time. One man said, "I have so many things to do that I think I'll get sleep off the list first!" He had a good point.

Taking off work one day out of seven might also seem like lost time, but it is not. The people who rest on the Lord's Day accomplish as much as the people who do not—and probably more. Remember not only to rest from your labor on the Lord's Day, but also to rest from planning your labor.

Enjoy being a good manager. Time management is not drudgery. See for yourself. Try spending a Saturday morning bumping from job to job with no particular plan. Linger over drinks of water, chat with everyone you meet, and stop to read the newspaper every time you pass it. Having had enough of that, take a little time at lunch to plan your afternoon. Set time limits for various chores, and see if you can stay within your schedule. Do you see how budgeting your time brightens the day? It is as good as an antidepressant.

Priceless Bank Account

If you had a bank that credited your account each morning with $86,400, that carried over no balance from day to day, that allowed you to keep no cash in your account, and that every evening canceled the amount you had failed to use during the day . . . what would you do? Draw out every cent, of course!

Well, you have such a bank, and its name is TIME.

Every morning, it credits you with 86,400 seconds.

Every night, it rules off—as lost—whatever of this you failed to invest for a good purpose.

It carries over no balances. It allows no overdrafts.

Each day, it opens a new account with you.

Each night, it burns the records of the day.

If you fail to use the day's deposits, the loss is yours.

There is no drawing against tomorrow.

You must live in the present—on today's deposits.

Invest it so as to get from it the utmost in health, happiness, and success!

—*Quarry Observer*

Consulting

"In the multitude of counsellors there is safety" (Proverbs 11:14). An English proverb says, "Two heads are better than one." You might be ever so intelligent, but you also have to be

> *"People who need the most advice seldom ask, and people who frequently ask seldom need the advice."*

informed. Even if no one were wiser than you, practically anyone could still tell you some things you did not know.

Do some reading. By reading, you can get advice from some of the most expert minds. Of course, not all books are equally good. Just because authors are eager to give advice does not qualify them to do so. On the other hand, many authors know a great deal about their chosen field and are justifiably confident that they have something worthwhile to say about it. Further, many authors have researched other books in preparing their own; so by reading, you are getting the cream from more than one person's thinking.

Do not let the subject embarrass you. Talking about money is hard for some people. I am not saying it is a general conversation piece or a way to break the ice with strangers. "How are you today?" still wins over "How's your checking account?" But notice that some individuals do not mind talking about facts and figures (to the right people), and they do it in a perfectly respectable way. You can too.

In fact, a friend says he is part of a financial circle in which each person is up-front with his finances, hiding nothing. At first, some people wanting to join the circle do not like this idea, and perhaps it is not a good idea for everyone. But it goes to show that with trusted people, even perfect frankness can be a workable arrangement.

In any case, you have to be frank enough to give your adviser a clear picture of what you want advice about. How can he give you good advice if you give him incomplete information?

Get professional advice. The trouble with getting advice from a doctor, lawyer, or Indian chief is that the advice is expensive. But ignorance is expensive too, sometimes even more costly than expert advice.

Even if you are a do-it-yourselfer, you might want to turn at least part of a project over to a professional. When one young man first started doing his own income taxes, he checked with an accountant to make sure he was doing it right. Being quite busy, the accountant was quite happy to look over his work, give a few tips, and let him do most of it himself.

Get brotherly advice. The professionals know their own field, but they might not know how people think in your church. "It's legal" might not be good enough for a brother who wants to know, "Is it *right?*" By the same token, "It's illegal" might not be perfectly true either, with a little more investigation.

Include the older brothers in the church. Remember Rehoboam, who forsook the old men's advice and followed the advice of the young men (1 Kings 12:8). Result: he lost most of his kingdom overnight.

> *"Keep the old trail well in sight until you know the new is right."*

Check with your father too. He might not know everything, but he certainly knows a few things. He remembers his successes and blunders, and he wants them to be steppingstones for you.

Consider salesmen's advice. It has often been pointed out that salesmen have a job to do—that is, to sell their product. Some salesmen will do this at the expense of their customers, so it is good to get a second opinion from a non-salesman.

On the other hand, you meet many good, reputable salesmen too. They want to serve you well, not only to keep you coming back but also to have the satisfaction of serving you well. Besides, they are experts in their line. You can learn much from what they have to say.

Take your time. Suppose you walk into a bank to open a checking account. To your bewilderment, the bank has four different kinds, and the lady at the desk begins describing them, pointing out each one on a glossy leaflet. Your first impulse might be inward irritation. "Why are you telling me all this? I just want a checking account. What have I walked into?"

Be patient. The lady is trying to meet your needs. Would you like to have a checking account that charges nothing but requires you to keep a hundred dollars or so in your account? Would you prefer not to worry about that minimum balance and pay a fee for each check instead? Listen carefully; a little extra time will not hurt you.

Be patient with yourself too. You can take in only so much advice in a single sitting. If you are not keeping up with the bank representative's flow of thought, ask her to repeat some things. Or repeat some things after her in her own words. If all the information she is giving you is starting to blur before your eyes, you might say, "May I take this information with me and think about these six options before I make a decision?"

You might also want to compare several different banks.

Beware "buyer's remorse." Schoolteachers know that first decisions are often the most likely to be correct. If a student writes an answer and then changes it, the new answer is often wrong. Likewise, once a person has bought a property or made a financial commitment, he is probably right—or at least not far wrong—to stick with his decision.

Somehow when you are rolling over in bed at 2:00 A.M., a recent decision can haunt you. The slightly raised eyebrow you saw yesterday undoes all the good advice you got before you made your decision.

This is not to say you must never call the other party back and ask for an honorable release. But unless you have come across some solid evidence that you are wrong, stick with your decision. Remember, if you change your mind, you will have to live with *that* decision too.

Do not take all the advice. You cannot do everything that everyone else says has worked for him. You would be charging off in a dozen different directions. Neither does everyone who offers advice expect you to follow it if you find something better to do. He is only trying to be helpful. He will be glad if things work out for you, regardless of what you finally decide.

Do take some of the advice. Accepting a person's advice shows respect for him, and it wins his respect in turn.

Keep in mind that if the advice reflects the experience of others, it is probably safe even if not very exciting. "Ask for the old paths" (Jeremiah 6:16). Be sure you understand the old system before you try something new. A new, untrodden path to

something good can turn out to be an old, well-trodden path to
something bad.

Do some things without "authorization" from others.
Most good advice you get comes as no surprise. You might even
have guessed what the other person would say. Very well; you
can often be your own counselor as Nehemiah was when he said,
"Then I consulted with myself" (Nehemiah 5:7).

Take final responsibility for your own decisions.
Sometimes after a person runs into financial difficulty, he agrees
to let a committee of several Christian brothers help him run his
affairs. This can be a great idea, but it has pitfalls.

Who makes the final decisions and takes responsibility for
them? Is it the person being helped, or is it the committee? If the
person is almost hopelessly in debt—and in debt to the committee
members, at that—he is no longer his own boss and had better
take the committee's advice as long as he is in debt. After all, it
is the committee's own money they are risking. "The borrower is
servant to the lender" (Proverbs 22:7).

On the other hand, if you basically want good advice and no
more, say so. Of course, then you are responsible for your own
decisions. You do not pay the committee for good advice nor blame
them for bad advice.

Committees can be self-perpetuating, much to the discomfort
of the brother who requested help in the first place. You might
want to establish the understanding that the committee will
automatically dissolve after a stipulated time, such as two years,
or after you have repaid 80 percent of your debt. You can always
extend the time, if you like.

Advice to Members of Financial Committees

Be kind. Be understanding. Your humble demeanor will help the brother in question to open up to you.

Be discreet with all information. Express no shock at what you learn. Let the brother keep his dignity and as much privacy as possible.

Do not throw a lot of ideas on the table until you have gathered the facts (make sure you get them all). Once the facts are gathered, the committee should retire to thoroughly discuss and weigh the situation, and then come back as a unified team with a workable solution. Be willing to make adjustments if necessary and if time proves it wise to do so.

Stay focused. Stick to the issues that caused the brother's financial problems in the first place. If he or his wife has been spending too lavishly on household luxuries, deal with that. On the other hand, if he was mismanaging in the barn, deal with that and try to stay out of the house. Avoid telling him how many flowers he may buy for his wife if that was never an issue. Again, if hog prices collapsed, deal with that and try to stay out of the barn. Do not assume he was lazy or careless when he was already working as hard as he could. (Admittedly, the issues may overlap.)

Know when your task is done. If you and the brother can set up a system of payments that slowly get him out of his hole, and if he is making the payments, it should not matter much to you what kind of sandwiches he takes to work in his lunch box.

Resist the tendency to let power go to your own head. Be especially wary if you have never been in a financial hole of your own. It is easy to become punitive and dictatorial. To help prevent this, maybe you should be accountable to the church ministry. After all, other church committees are.

2. Earning

The Difference Between Wealth and Money

"Not slothful in business" (Romans 12:11) really means "Not slothful in busyness." The Bible teaches this for good reason.

All wealth is created by work. Can you think of any exceptions? You might say that your money in the bank can generate wealth in the form of interest and that that process is not work. No, maybe there is no work on *your* part. But you know very well that the banker does not stash your money in a safe, hoping that when he comes back he will find that it has given birth to interest.

What does he do with it? He lends the money to other people who use it to buy—a dump truck, for instance. The dump truck gives someone the opportunity to work. With the profits from that work, the truck owner pays his loan back to the bank along with interest, and out of the interest the bank pays you.

You might say that not everyone borrows to buy work equipment. Don't some people borrow to buy luxury items that create no wealth? Yes, but even those luxury items were made by labor, using equipment that was made by still more labor.

You might say that inflation can create wealth. After all, if you can buy a property and then sell it ten years later for twice as much, is that not the creation of wealth? But the truth is that the buyer lost just as much as you gained. So the net result is the same. No wealth was created.

It might be even more accurate to say that you yourself lost

By *wealth* we do not mean "purple and fine linen" but simply prosperity and human well-being, the kind of thing Paul described when he advised the former thief to "labour, working with his hands the thing which is good, that he may have to give to him that needeth" (Ephesians 4:28). The dictionary calls this kind of wealth "goods and resources having economic value."[1]

as much as you gained. You need all those extra dollars to buy another property of the same value. Inflation means more dollars but less value per dollar. One is reminded of the boy who amused himself by standing in a bucket and pulling up on it with his hands, trying to lift himself from the floor. One time he thought he was getting it accomplished—his hands were coming up! But no, he was standing in a rusty bucket, and his feet were pushing through the bottom. Always, one force balanced the other; the net result was no gain. And the same truth applies to inflation.

Although it takes work to create *wealth*, creating *money* is a different matter. The government does it in several ways. One of the most obvious is to print paper money and to mint coins. Another way is for the Federal Reserve System to supply banks with money by check. The figure on the check is backed only by the authority of the government and is limited only by the common sense of Federal Reserve officials.[2]

Still another way to create money—well, let us illustrate. Mr. Jones borrows a thousand dollars from the bank and uses it to buy a garden tiller. The thousand dollars is then in the hands of the implement dealer, who puts it in the bank. Mr. McCormick then walks into the bank, borrows the thousand dollars that the implement dealer deposited, and also buys a garden tiller. The implement dealer once again puts it in the bank. Now Mr. Carter walks into the bank . . . Do you see what is happening? Suddenly one thousand dollars is three thousand dollars because it was borrowed several times.

Actually, we are oversimplifying. The law does not allow a bank to lend 100 percent of the money it takes in. If a bank should lend the same money over and over indefinitely, things would eventually collapse. A community cannot borrow itself rich. Still, a bank may lend enough so that the money it takes in is multiplied a number of times.

Sometimes a bank may lend a higher percentage of the money it holds, sometimes a lower percentage, depending on federal regulations. This is one way the government controls the economy, sometimes loosening the controls to stoke the fires of prosperity a little, sometimes tightening controls to keep inflation from running away.

Banks keep on hand only a fraction of the money they would need to pay out if all their customers asked for it at once. This method is used in a fractional reserve banking system. Bank customers do not panic (as in days past) over the knowledge that not everyone's money is sitting in the local bank, waiting to be withdrawn. They know that the government insures their deposits.

Once again, money is the appearance of wealth, the representation of wealth, but it is not wealth itself. If that is not clear, write out a check for a thousand dollars and then burn it. Were you richer after the check was written out? No. Were you poorer after you burned it? No.

Money in the form of cash is not much different. It is like a check written out by someone else. You would be poorer if you burned a friend's check made out to you, but he would not be. No wealth was destroyed. Likewise, you would be poorer if you burned a paper dollar, but the country as a whole would not be, not even if you burned a million dollars. In fact, other people would be as well off or better because their paper dollars would be worth a little more without yours. Cash is not wealth; it only represents wealth.

Not even gold and silver are wealth. They too are based on the fact of human acceptance. Gold has been accepted as wealth so long that we naturally think of it that way. But suppose you offer gold to pay your taxes tomorrow and the officer turns up his nose and says, "Copper is the medium of exchange now." What could you do? Could you say, "Fine; I'll eat my gold"? You might argue that gold does have some value for practical uses, which is true, but that is not the value we are talking about.

However, if you accidentally burned down a million-dollar warehouse, you would be destroying real wealth. Now we are talking about actual food, or clothing, or books, or furniture, or whatever might be stored in a warehouse, plus the value of the warehouse itself. People would be worse off because fewer things of value would exist.

By the same principle, some labor produces intangible wealth. The knowledge a teacher imparts to a student is a kind of wealth, even though you cannot burn it down in a warehouse. So is the good advice that some counselors give.

In any case, the work that creates wealth is hard work. There is no substitute for raw energy, and there is no substitute for the willingness to work even when one is tired, bored, old, cold, hungry, hot, or feeling just plain lazy.

The nearest thing I can think of to wealth without work is blackberries growing along a hedgerow. But even then, you have to pick them. Picking them is work—maybe a pleasant kind of work—but work nonetheless. The same principle applies to the wealth of our mines and forests. And any farmer knows that farming takes work despite the fact that God makes the crops grow for free.

> *If every laborer in the nation were paid a thousand dollars an hour, you would not be able to buy any more than you are already getting, because someone would have to produce goods at that wage before you could buy them.*

Work makes the world go around. According to one story, a man dreamed that he got up in the morning to find that nothing was working. The electric lights, the faucet, the milk that should have been delivered to his door—nothing. He could not shave. He could not get his breakfast. Walking outside to investigate further, he noticed that no buses or taxis were running and that everything looked strangely deserted. Just then he saw a boy running down the street and shouted, "Hey, what's the trouble?" The boy replied, "Haven't you heard? Everyone has inherited a million dollars! Nobody has to work!"

More About Creating Wealth

Although labor is valuable, one should not get the impression that heavy, oxlike labor is the complete answer. Not all labor creates wealth. One can work just as hard at making mud pies as at making cherry pies, but the final value is not the same.

Even white-collar labor may or may not be a wealth producer. Speculators on Wall Street are working as hard as anyone, but they are not creating wealth. They are just rearranging it.

Since some labor creates a great deal of wealth, some creates less, and some creates none, would it not make sense to engage in the kind of labor that creates real wealth and leaves people better off?

For instance, with your bare hands, you can create only a limited amount of wealth. You can sell your time but little else. After you equip yourself with tools and a pickup truck, you can produce more and are more valuable to your employer. He should be glad to pay you more, and you should feel comfortable in accepting it.

With experience and growing skill, you are worth more again. Time for another raise! But it is best to let the boss think of it first. He probably will, especially if he has ever told you, "We don't work harder, we work smarter."

Finally, if you learn business management, you can go into business for yourself. Of course, your boss will be sorry to see you go, but he and you should both be comfortable with the thought that he got his money's worth out of you already. With the Lord's blessing, you are in a position to create more wealth than ever before.

What am I saying by all of this? We should be happy working wherever we are, but move up the scale of usefulness as it seems appropriate. Paul's advice to servants was, "Art thou called being a servant? care not for it: but if thou mayest be made free, use it rather" (1 Corinthians 7:21).

Are there any limits to this concept of moving up the scale of usefulness? Certainly. Some businessmen assume that the bigger their business, the better. After all, they can serve more people that way. But often such people's spiritual lives go into decline, and even worse, their examples do serious harm to their children. As Jesus said, "How hardly shall they that have riches enter into the kingdom of God!" (Mark 10:23). And even more hardly shall their children enter in!

Then too, many professionals carry this concept to such a degree that they charge exorbitant fees for their services. Such fees are not always as exorbitant as the man in the waiting room may think, since the professional must pay for his office, his assistants, his receptionist, and so on. But in many cases, the bills for professional services are higher than what the professional would charge if he loved his neighbor as himself.

The average worker in a Western civilization produces four or five times as much as the average worker in an undeveloped country.[3] That is impressive, is it not? But what is the American worker producing in his state-of-the-art factory, powered by electricity and operated by robots and computers? We all need "food and raiment," as the apostle Paul said, and we may safely add various comforts to his simple list. But American workers also produce green hair dye, cheap paperbacks, various knickknacks and ornaments, and all the other clutter in the aisles of department stores which you pass by with barely a glance. If we subtract that from the wealth we think we are producing, we will not be very far above the cross-legged African who does woodcarving by hand.

Choosing a Vocation

"How shall I make a living?" is one of the three greatest decisions you will ever make. The other two are "What kind of person shall I marry?" and "What kind of person shall I be?" These two are not our subject, of course, though they come into the picture.*

To properly answer the question "How shall I make a living?" we will need to consider several related questions. Here they are, not necessarily in the order of importance.

What do people need? For example, should you work in the tobacco industry? No, because people do not need those health hazards and that air pollution. Should you work at manufacturing land mines? No, because people do not need to get their feet blown off.

The question becomes more vexatious when you consider producing something good that is already in plentiful supply. Do people need your milk when there is already a milk surplus? Do they need your jam when they can already buy Smucker's or Western Family or Danish Orchards or Robertson's or Dickinson's or Knott's or Welch's or Mary McCrank's? Do they need your mustard when other producers are already making aqua-colored

---

* For another helpful chapter on this subject, see "What Should You Work?" in David G. Burkholder's book, *Young Man, Be Strong* (Crockett, KY: Rod and Staff Publishers, 1988).

> "Many of our occupations include a measure of dealing with the vanities of men. Carpenters sometimes build elaborate houses. Landscapers might do fancy, ornamental work around buildings. Printers at times print eye-catching promotional pieces. Mechanics repair vehicles that may have a sporty or classy image. Although we might do things for others which we would not do for ourselves, we must be careful lest we are influenced to think that these things are right for us to have. We should also be careful to never encourage the vanities of man for our own financial gain."[4]

mustard to tease children to tease their parents to buy it?

Maybe we could put it like this: It is all right to produce something good that people would buy anyway. Milk is good; jam is good; mustard is good. People need a certain amount of it. If they are going to buy it from someone, why not buy it from you? If you refuse to enter a field of endeavor until no one else is in it, you might be waiting a long time.

Still, it is satisfying to find a niche in the market. Maybe you can produce something a little different from the usual. People like homemade items—your own particular kind of mustard or jam, for example. Certain customers might want goat's milk or duck eggs because they have a child who is allergic to cow's milk or chicken eggs.

Of course, the most satisfying thing you can do is to help people with really urgent needs. Some people, even in North America, are short on food, clothing, and shelter. Why not go into a business that serves them?

That is a wonderful thought—until a second thought hits. If only there were money in it! Unfortunately, the people with the most needs have the least money. If you sell luxuries to the rich, you can make good money. There is more money in building swimming pools than in building houses, and more money in building elaborate houses than in building simple ones. Selling Bibles in North America is more profitable than translating the Bible and

> *Although working for the rich can be lucrative, there are exceptions. One painter spray-painting the outside of a house door accidentally got some spray inside the door on the carpet. He ended up having to pay for a complete re-installation of all the carpet in the house. That misfortune put him out of business.*

putting it into the hands of a remote Indian tribe in Peru.

So here is the dilemma. In many instances, the more useful your business is to mankind, the less money you make at it. Yet you need money. How else can you be useful?

Your first thought might be to compromise. Maybe you could make jam one day a week so you have money to write books on the other days. Jam makers may smile at how simple this sounds, but people do sometimes support a calling by working at a part-time occupation that makes more money.

On the other hand, let us remember that we do not have to solve this problem all by ourselves. We belong to a greater body. Maybe we could go into full-time Christian service and let others supply our needs. Some people might be delighted to help us out.

A person in full-time Christian service has plenty of time to give to the Lord but wishes he could give more money. A successful Christian businessman has plenty of money to give to the Lord but wishes he could give more time. Why not bring their resources together?

"For I mean not that other men be eased, and ye burdened: but by an equality, that now at this time your abundance may be a supply for their want, that their abundance also may be a supply for your want: that there may be equality: as it is written, He that had gathered much had nothing over; and he that had gathered little had no lack" (2 Corinthians 8:13–15). The apostle Paul had another setting from ours in mind when he wrote this, but the principle remains the same.

So far nothing has been said about the rightness of Christian service as compared with ordinary labor. Some people feel sensitive about this. Someone asked a teacher what he had been doing over the summer, and he replied in apologetic tones, "I was working for mammon."

Actually, working with wood, concrete, cows, apples, dishes, and vacuum cleaners can be perfectly healthy and honorable for a Christian. Jesus Himself was a carpenter longer than a teacher. "Every legitimate vocation is equally acceptable before God: there are no secular and sacred divisions in life for the Christian."[5] But we do have a problem if we cling to the old familiar things when the Lord calls us to do as He did—to lay down our carpenter tools in favor of a new calling.

Jesus said, "But seek ye first the kingdom of God, and his righteousness; and all these things shall be added unto you" (Matthew 6:33).

What do people want? People need to eat more spinach, right? Yes, indeed, especially if you are a spinach farmer. The next question is, Do they want it? Deciding what people need is one thing; getting them to buy it is quite another.

The formula, then, is to start with what people need—and want—and will buy. Then work backward, and ask yourself how you will produce and market it. It is human nature to start at the other end and ask, "What would I like to produce?" Then: "How will I market it?" Then: "Oh, by the way, who will buy it?"

One summer a young fellow thought he would raise sweet potatoes. So he used his neighbor's vacant lot, paid another neighbor to plow it up, and bought sweet potato plants. The project did fairly well, and he got a pile of sweet potatoes.

Then he started looking around for people who wanted the little creatures! He called different stores and soon found out that if they wanted sweet potatoes at all, they preferred yellow ones—nice-shaped ones like the kind they could get from New Jersey. His were red, and the shapes were—well—interesting. One or two stores took some potatoes, but he still had a pile.

Finally he called his uncle, who had a truck route business, selling eggs and vegetables and things like that. His uncle kindly took them off his hands and even paid him something for them. But afterward, his father remarked, "We sort of hung them on him, didn't we." The lesson, we hope, was well learned.

What can I produce? By the time you reach adulthood, you have probably worked in a number of fields and know what you can do well. Perhaps you have tried swinging a hammer, raising vegetables, selling sweet corn, feeding calves, fixing appliances, tutoring schoolchildren, writing letters, and doing desk work. Occasionally a hobby will lead a person into his lifework, but usually his guide is some familiar line of labor.

Thankfully, what you can do well and what you like to do are usually not too far apart. This brings us to our next question.

What kind of job would be fulfilling? This question has a practical side because you naturally do more of what you enjoy. The housepainter who would rather paint than eat will cut his lunch break short so he can go back to painting. The painter who does not like his job will seldom work overtime, nor will he work as fast and as well as the happy painter. Finding fulfillment in one's job does have a connection to earning a living.

However, this is not an extremely urgent question. Sometimes after he is out of school, a young person will take a job to fill the gap while he decides what to do long-term. "It's not something I want to do all my life," said one young man, but he did not appear to be suffering in the meantime. Remember, satisfaction depends not on doing what one likes to do, but on liking what one has to do.

> A young man once told a professor that what he wanted most to do in life was to write.
> "But you will starve," said the professor.
> "I don't care if I do," said the young man.
> "Then," said the older man, "you will succeed."[6]

Will it be spiritually helpful or harmful? Some jobs, like thinning peaches all by yourself in the middle of an orchard, give you plenty of time to reflect and meditate. But then the wrong kind of thoughts can come, too. Maybe you need a job that keeps your mind more occupied.

Some jobs involve working alongside other people. This is fine if they are the kind of people who draw the best out of you. But not everyone does. Maybe—but not just maybe—you should find a job that keeps you out of the world's worst influences.

Some jobs—well, perhaps we have already made the point clear. Here are a number of questions you can ask yourself along this line.

Will I have time to support church activities? Maybe you cannot make it to every church cleaning, but prayer meeting is a different matter.

Will the occupation help my testimony, or mar it? There might be nothing wrong with housesitting for your rich neighbor, but how will people feel about your living in his mansion? There might be nothing wrong with driving shiny sports cars from one car lot to another, but how will it impress those who see *you* doing it? People have opinions about such matters, and it might be easier

Checking the classified ads might land you a job. But it is a shot in the twilight if you are looking for a job with an environment safe for a Christian. Then too, be cautious about companies that advertise for employees week after week. If their employees are happy, why should the company always be needing to fill vacancies? Feel free to get in touch with reputable employers even if they are not advertising for help.

to adjust your ways than to adjust their thinking.

Am I looking for a trade or for a profession? Many conservative people are involved in trades; they are skilled laborers, such as electricians, plumbers, carpenters, mechanics, and farmers. A profession is different. A doctor or lawyer has studied much longer and paid much more for his training than a tradesman has. There is nothing intrinsically wrong with being a professional (that is, in becoming highly trained in a responsible field). However, several problems present themselves.

—Being a professional tends to elevate a person (in other people's eyes, if not in his own) and to put him in a class by himself.

—It gives him an identity that can be more obvious than his identity as a Christian.

—It offers him a fellowship among other professionals which can draw him away from his brothers in the faith.

—It tends to occupy his time and attention too much.

Will the job be good for my family? Again we have a few related questions.

Can I get home every night? Long-distance truck driving is notorious for ruining homes. Not only does the trucker face unique temptations, but his family goes fatherless, perhaps for several nights running.

Will this occupation expose my children to bad influences? For instance, do you want to tend a farmers' market stall if you cannot keep your children busy there and they want to explore the market? Do you want to sell Jingle products if it involves holding many meetings where your children play with other children from all kinds of backgrounds? One bathroom joke told to a seven-year-old can cling to his memory for the rest of his life. We cannot avoid all of this, but we must make it our business to keep it at a minimum.

Can my children work alongside me in this vocation? Some fathers and their families are unfortunate along this line. Father's job is not wrong, but there is not much the children can do to help. If such is your lot, maybe you can make up for it by working in the garden or shop with them in the evening. But if you choose a vocation where your little ones can run in and out and where your older ones can help, you and your family will be richer in more things than money.

Is there money in it? Although you should choose a vocation you like, you really do need to consider money. Suppose someone comes up with the brilliant idea of generating electricity to make a living. He is young and strong, and he has an exercise bicycle and a generator! He will hook up the generator to the power lines and sell electricity to the system. What a wonderful idea! Why hadn't anyone else thought of this before?

But then he learns that a bicycle generator produces about enough power to illuminate one light bulb. Cautiously he asks an electrician friend, "How much does the electricity cost to operate one light bulb?"

"Oh," says his friend, "about a penny an hour. Why?"

One brother thought refinishing furniture would be a good idea. What better way to save things than to fix up battered old chairs? So he refinished a rocking chair and a few other items only to learn that the process took a long while. He could not get enough money out of it to pay for his time.

Later he dropped in on an old gentleman who had some refinished furniture for sale, sitting out in his driveway. The man told him the same thing. He was basically retired, had the money and the time, and could afford to refinish items and still sell them fairly cheap. But he would never try to make a living at it.

Of course, some people refinish furniture as a business, but they charge for it too; so most of the pieces that pass through their hands are antiques. That is a different story and raises questions about how involved you should be in a business that often involves inflated* prices.

---

* A polite word for "outrageous."

"There are some over-pious Christian people who think if you take any profit on anything you sell, you are an unrighteous man On the contrary, you would be a criminal to sell goods for less than they cost. You have no right to do that. You cannot trust a man with your money who cannot take care of his own. . . . I have no more right to sell goods without making a profit on them than I have to overcharge [the customer] dishonestly beyond what they are worth. But I should so sell each bill of goods that the person to whom I sell shall make as much as I make."[7]

Even if you choose a promising vocation, it will not pay if you fail to charge enough. One young contractor said he used to do a job for someone, look at the bill he calculated, and think, "This is too much!" So he would knock some off the bill.

At the end of the year, he looked at the final income figure. So *this* was all he had earned? Something would need to change.

Maybe he should have guessed that all along. What had he gotten for handing customers low bills? Comments like "Oh, I thought the bill would be higher."

Should you be self-employed? Remember what Jesus said about sitting down to count the cost. Here are a few considerations to help you in your counting.

Do you have plenty of energy? Talk to the owner of any store, even a small one, and see how much time he spends on the business after everyone else has gone home.

Do you enjoy record keeping? Running one's own business involves a fair amount of office work.

Do you know your business? Someone asked a friend if he had once been a mechanic, and he replied, "I tried to pretend I was." That is one reason why the state requires professionals and a growing number of craftsmen to be certified. In theory at least, certification helps keep amateurs off the market and helps protect customers from unpleasant surprises.

Even if your job does not require certification, work for someone else in the business before you assume that you know enough to run it yourself. Take painting, for example. Anyone can swing a paintbrush, right? Still, before you go into the painting business, let someone else be your boss. He can show you little tricks about masking, spraying, rolling, sanding, and filling nail holes that can make you much more efficient. This can be critical in a highly competitive business world that puts a premium on getting in, getting done (right), and getting out.

Are you confident by nature? Sometimes an overly cautious person fails to take up a new enterprise, or he quickly backs out of it because he thinks a certain new skill is "over my head" or "out of my field." A more confident person enters new territory and masters it with time and patience.

Are you familiar with state and county laws that pertain to the trade you are considering? For example, do you need a contractor's license?

Do you have enough money to get started? Even starting up house painting might cost more than what you expected. A body-shop owner will need a great deal. "A rule of thumb is that you should have, or at least have ready access to, one-third of the required capital."[8]

Will you be crushed by overhead costs? See if you can work out of your home to avoid the high cost of renting an office or a shop. Of course, this advice does not always apply. You cannot be a tractor mechanic in your basement. Just remember that shop rental bills are as sure as sure can be, and you had better have a good idea how you will pay those bills before they land on your desk.

Have you included taxes in your calculations? Many people forget to do that.

How fast can you reasonably expect the business to reach the point of sustaining itself? Suppose you want to get into the business of making minibarns. Will the world make a beaten path to your door just because you hang up a sign that says "Open for Business"? Will you not need to make some sample barns and have them on display at a number of public places before people even know that your business exists? You will also need to do things like displaying your business cards at hardware stores, listing your business in the yellow pages, and getting a toll-free telephone number.

Remember too that just before Christmas, people will have their minds on things other than buying minibarns. How will you live in the meantime? In other words, have you worked out some kind of realistic budget in which you subtract your business expenses from your business income and find out if the amount left is enough? "A common rule of thumb is that you should expect to go for at least one full year with no income at all!"[9]

Are you prepared for the trauma of failure? Many businesses fail; indeed most of them fold up within a few years. Probably you knew that already. But what you might have failed to think of is this: when a business goes down the drain, it often takes the owner's life savings along with it.

Can you distinguish the feel of failure from the real thing? Maybe what feels like failure is not the end of the road after all, and you are just too easily discouraged. A salesman put it something like this: "You walk into a business and leave a sample of your product. A few weeks later, you come back and discover that the manager is in a meeting somewhere and can't talk to you. You come back later and discover that he hasn't even checked out your product yet. You might have to come back the fifth or sixth time before you get somewhere." That is discouraging, but the salesman who said this was nevertheless making a success of his job.

The other side of the matter is, can you distinguish the feel of success from the real thing? Some bright-eyed entrepreneurs keep seeing success just around the corner when they should actually cut their losses and get out.

Here are a few other considerations.

The ability to manage an enterprise should be tested before it is expanded through the use of borrowed funds. If this is not possible, the idea should at least be tested on paper, using conservative figures. Counsel should also be sought from those who have had experience in this particular enterprise.

High-risk types of enterprises should be avoided. What may look like a quick dollar may very easily end up as a financial disaster. Records must be kept, performance evaluated, and the resources available for production must be regularly reviewed.

Debts must be kept in line with income repayment capacity. Income must be sufficient to meet operating expenses, debt retirement, family living expenses, and the Lord's work, with some built-in cushion for the unexpected that may come.

A dependable lender should be selected. The terms and conditions of the loan should be completely evaluated and understood. It is always profitable to ask counsel from someone who is experienced in making loans.[10]

The same article says:

The period following World War II until 1980 was known as a time of inflation. This inflationary period caused people to become more reckless in investing and making financial commitments. Many people violated the principle of safe monetary investments and depended on inflation to help them through. Banks and lending institutions were freely loaning monies without always thoroughly investigating the feasibility of the loan.

The last number of years has been a period of less inflation and, in fact, a period of deflation of some financial holdings, which brings a decrease of equity. Profits have decreased considerably, even to the extent that some people in business are taking a loss. One reason for this loss may be that they are too dependent on borrowed money, which obligates them to large amounts of interest that consume the greater part of their income.

In some situations the financial stress has made it impossible to continue in business. The business must be dissolved only to discover that the equity value has declined to the extent that the holdings are no more solvent. In some situations large unpaid debts are left without any more resource to draw from. In some situations it will mean the person must appropriate a large part of his income toward that debt for many years, which causes a very undesirable situation for the family.[11]

Once the business is up and running, will it bring you enough income? Five hundred dollars a month is a tidy little sum—for a sideline business. It is not a tidy sum at all if it's your only source of income and you are trying to raise a family in Massachusetts.

Are you being realistic? There is a child within all of us that likes the glitter of being in business for oneself. Can you resist this impulse in favor of larger considerations? Do you think you will also be able in the future to resist the pressure to expand your business unduly?

Will the work be steady and secure? We can, of course,

worry too much about work security. Our security is finally in God, not in jobs.

For example, suppose you are offered a job in a chair shop, where the income is good, the work is wholesome, and you get to work with other Christians. Should you turn it down just because during the Great Depression the manufacturing of durable goods went into decline? Of course not. Other considerations are more important than that.

Still, a little common sense about job security only makes common sense. Some occupations are the first to wilt when prosperity wanes. All other things being equal, a job in the service industries (for example, repair work or schoolteaching) is probably more secure than what working as an interior decorator for the World Trade Center was on September 10, 2001.

But once again, do not spend a lot of time worrying about whether a job is secure. If you choose a job that is a service to mankind and run it right, you will probably be fairly secure.

What do I mean by "run it right"? Well, even a good business can be managed wrong. You can run it so close to the edge that as soon as the economy takes a dip, you are in trouble. One housebuilder was prospering nicely but overextended himself. He might have gotten away with it, but about that time the economy slackened. He ended up having to sell his house and move his family into his parents' home.

Running it right also means putting enough effort into it. "He becometh poor that dealeth with a slack hand: but the hand of the diligent maketh rich" (Proverbs 10:4). Producing a quality product and delivering it when you promise it, will win you a good name and the loyalty of your customers.

The most dangerous way to run a business wrong is to be in a hurry for money. You will tend to take too many risks. Your sure-fire plans are likely to backfire and cost you more than you can afford—much more. "He that hasteth to be rich hath an evil eye, and considereth not that poverty shall come upon him" (Proverbs 28:22).

Furthermore, if you are in a hurry for money, you are likely to jump into a given field too late. Recently a friend told me that catfish farms in Mississippi had been doing fine and making more money than other kinds of farming. Want to jump into catfish farming?

Wait a minute. He also said the price for a pound of catfish had been dropping to the point that farmers were getting fifty cents a pound. They figured that they would need to get forty-five cents a pound just to break even. Maybe you should drop the catfish farming idea and find a job as a catfish farm auctioneer.

By the same token, there is little point these days in starting up a llama farm. The day of llamas has probably come and gone. And do not ask me what the newest hot item is. It will not be hot by the time this book is published anyway.

Will other businesses be hurt? You should not be too sensitive about starting up a business just because someone else already has a business like it a few miles down the road. As a community grows, new businesses are part of life. In fact, a new shoe store close to an existing shoe store might increase business for both of them because word gets around that in that corner of town there are two shoe stores and not just one.

> *"Do not be afraid to let the other fellow make a dollar."*

The main consideration is not the fact that you are starting a new business but the way you will run it. As a new business owner, eager for customers, you might cut prices so low that neither you nor your competitor makes a decent profit. That is not fair.

A book for beekeepers says, "[The honey producer] should be careful to consult the market to learn what the retail prices are and sell it at retail. It is always a mistake to cut prices under the grocer, because if the beekeeper ever antagonizes that individual he may shut off an important outlet for his honey some seasons when he cannot sell his entire product from his home. In any event, it is always wise to cooperate with the local dealer as far as possible."[12]

Any principle on either side can be taken too far. You want to be kind to your competitor/colleague, but at the same time, "competition is the lifeblood of trade." It helps to keep quality up and prices down. Competition is a way of being kind to your customer.

To Those Who Might Become Farmers

Today the plight of many farmers is very much being discussed. No one seems to have a simple solution. There are victims of natural disasters, victims of changes in the economy, those who are overextended, and others who are facing immediate problems. There are also those young farmers who are trying to decide what to do in the future. Should they start up farming?

The following are some considerations for young people thinking about farming.

1. Are you ready to face the challenges that lie ahead? There is nothing wrong with challenges. We had them in the 1950s when I started farming, but unwise decisions probably did not have as severe consequences as they do today.

2. Are you ready to accept the disciplines and hard knocks that you will experience for at least the first few years? These are things that cannot be delegated to someone else. They prepare us for the long haul, but sometimes they are really difficult.

3. Be ready to put in an honest day's work. This doesn't guarantee a successful operation, but it helps. It also sets a good example for the children.

4. Be a good steward of the soil. Determine that the land you turn over to future generations will be as good as or better and more productive than it was when you received it.

5. Try to find a neighbor who will buy certain pieces of machinery in partnership with you. (My Christian neighbor and I bought a baler in partnership 30 years ago and worked together on this part of farming).

6. Try to economize in purchasing machinery. Good, serviceable, used machinery can help bridge the gap for a few years.

7. Drought, floods, livestock diseases (it seems there are more now than a few years ago), family medical bills, low market prices, and high interest rates are all uncertainties which enter the picture.

8. Don't expect the government to be of any help if you need help. In the past, farm programs subsidized (tax breaks, huge payments for not planting) the big farmer and penalized (payments were not worthwhile even if he could take the payment with a clear conscience, because they were too small or the farm operation was diversified and it didn't fit in) the family farm.

9. Farming today is much more complex and competitive than when I started 35 years ago. It will be more so in the future.

10. One of the myths of our society is that "big is better." Grow only as much as you can handle and need. There are many out there who are family farmers, happy and content. "But godliness with contentment is great gain. For we brought nothing into this world, and it is certain we can carry nothing out. And having food and raiment let us be therewith content" (1 Timothy 6:6–8).

11. If financial success eventually comes your way, be sure to remember the words of God to the Israelites in Deuteronomy 8:10–14: "When thou hast eaten and art full, then thou shalt bless the LORD thy God for the good land which he hath given thee. Beware that thou forget not the LORD thy God, in not keeping his commandments, and his judgments, and his statutes, which I command thee this day: lest when thou hast eaten and art full, and hast built goodly houses, and dwelt therein; and when thy herds and thy flocks multiply, and thy silver and thy gold is multiplied, and all that thou hast is multiplied; then thine heart be lifted up, and thou forget the LORD thy God, which brought thee forth out of the land of Egypt, from the house of bondage."

These eleven points are suggested not to discourage anyone from farming, but rather to take an overall view of what it will involve. Many are going to accept these challenges and go at it with a determined effort. Some of us who have reached the time in life to phase out our operation should rent our land to these young farmers and not make them compete in bidding for land against those who have so much.[13]

Network Marketing

Practically everyone has heard of Amway products, and many have heard names like Shaklee, Market America, and so on. At the same time, many of us have heard warnings against being involved in pyramid schemes. Should we then get involved in network marketing (also known as multi-level marketing)? Is that a pyramid scheme?

The answer is not as simple as it looks. First we need to define pyramid schemes and find network marketing either innocent or guilty. Even if we find it innocent, we should still look at other questions involved.

First, a little history.

Back in 1943, a company called Nutralite Food Supplement Corporation came forward with a program encouraging its salespeople to build their own little sales organizations. They were to recruit other salesmen—friends, neighbors, relatives— and in this way expand the sales network.

Of course, recruiting others called for a reward. Why else would a salesman recruit competition? So the system rewarded a person by skimming off for him a little money from what his recruits sold and even from what his recruit's recruits sold. This meant that a lot of money went into the pockets of the salesmen at different levels. On the other hand, the money did not go into maintaining a store.

The idea caught on slowly at first, then rapidly. But as often happens with new ideas, people abused it. They would buy into a business with the idea that they could recruit other people who would also buy into the business. Money kept being handed up the line to the people at the top. It was all a money game; in some cases the business did not even have a legitimate product. Predictably, people at the top got rich and people near the bottom of the chain got burned. Some lost everything they had.

Finally the Federal Trade Commission (FTC) stepped in, brought suit against some companies, and shut them down. Still, the question had not been completely settled. What was a legitimate business, and what was not?

In 1975 the FTC took the giant Amway itself to court. After four years, the judges handed down their decision. Yes, network marketing is legitimate, but it does need to meet certain standards. Basically, network marketing is acceptable by law if it meets the following tests.

—Does it offer a real product? Simply sending money up the levels of a chain is not acceptable.

—Does it set a fair price? Maybe a real product is there; but if the price is exorbitant, the end result is not much different from having no real product at all.

—Are sales personnel paid on the basis of actual sales? Merely recruiting salesmen, without actually getting the product into the hands of customers, is a racket, pure and simple.

—Are salesmen encouraged not to engage in "inventory loading"? Companies must not require salespeople to buy a large amount of merchandise with no option to sell it back to the company.

—Are the earnings realistic? If a salesman is offered too much in proportion to his sales, sooner or later he or the company will suffer.

Pyramid schemes fail this test. But if a network arrangement can answer "yes" to every question, it is not a pyramid scheme, as most knowledgeable people would define it. The concept of network marketing is legal essentially because it is a valid system of doing business.

One question remains! If network marketing is good as a business concept, does it also keep good company? What are the involvements? Are they innocent too?

Here are some considerations.

Social contacts. One woman remembers spending many evenings in her childhood playing with other children of all kinds. There is nothing wrong with having friends of all kinds, but too much socializing with friends who have relatively low values is not good for children—or adults either.

Family life. One can have too little social contact with his own family. Of course, running other businesses can also be detrimental to family life, but network marketing seems especially hard on evening family time.

> *A friend's comment:*
> Able-bodied Christian people should entirely avoid this type of business. It may have some place with the handicapped or aged.

Avarice. The common word for this is *greed!* Something quickens the pulse when you get those glossy brochures saying how much other people are earning every month, and suggesting that you can do the same. Have the laws that regulate the industry screened out the something-for-nothing mentality? Not a chance!

Competition for loyalties. Most network companies are not satisfied merely to serve as a selling program. They try to minister to the whole man. They pressure their salesmen to attend weekend seminars at distant locations. They hold nondenominational worship services. They offer social life to lonely people.

The result? A person can easily become dissatisfied with his church relationships and even his marriage because his relationship with the company seems to offer something better. It offers new values for the old ones that the individual should have kept.

Another point is that most network marketers are not from a conservative Christian background, as most readers of this book are. Predictably, they are not nearly as conservative and careful in their man–woman relationships either.

Don't traditional businesses present these same traps? No doubt some of them do. But just because network marketing has no monopoly on problems does not mean it has no problems. We should avoid traps wherever we find them.

By all this, we are not passing judgment on everyone involved in network programs. These cautions are simply here to help you judge the programs themselves lest you reinvent the blunders that others have made.

Chain Letters

The following is an unbelievably blatant example of a pyramid scheme. Obviously nothing of value is being produced. But it just arrived in our mailbox today, so evidently people are still falling for this kind of thing. Here it is, except that names have been changed.

PLEASE READ THIS ENTIRE LETTER BEFORE ACTING ON IT
This letter is legal: Refer to Title 18, Section 1302, U.S. Postal Service Regulations.

HELLO.
My name is Harold Printz. In September 1991, my car was repossessed and the bill collectors were hounding me like you wouldn't believe. I was laid off my job and my unemployment ran out. In 1992, my family and I went on a 10-day cruise. Then I built a new house in Virginia, and I will never have to work again.
In 1991, I received a letter in the mail telling me how to earn $50,000

anytime I wanted to. Of course I was skeptical. But because I was desperate and had nothing to lose, I gave it a try. I promised that any money I received would be shared with others. Today . . . I consider myself both fortunate and well-off.

During the first year, I earned over $200,000 and then became a millionaire the following year. This is a legitimate business opportunity, and it's legal. It works every time. I have never failed to earn less than $50,000 each time. It does not require you to sell anything, to go to meetings, or come into contact with any people. In fact, the only time you have to leave your home is to mail your letters. If you have always believed that someday you would get a good break, your time has finally arrived. Now it's up to you! Simply follow the instructions exactly and in good faith. In 20 to 60 days, you will receive up to $50,000 in cash.

1. IMMEDIATELY mail $2.00 cash to each of the names below. Place it between a folded piece of paper for security.

2. Remove the top name in the number-one spot, move the others up and place your name and address in the number-six spot.

3. Make 200 to 500 copies of this letter with your name and address in the number-six spot. (The more copies you mail, the more money you'll make.)

4. Get a list of names from the list company "NATIONAL NAMES LISTS" PO BOX 20—(MAILING LISTS) RICHVILLE, PA 17123. ($35) for 200 names or ($70) for 500 names. You must pay by money order.

5. While waiting for your mailing list to arrive (about 7–10 days), place the copies of your letters in stamped envelopes. Do not put a return address on the envelopes.

6. When your mailing list arrives, it will come in the form of laser-quality, peel-and-stick labels. Place the labels on the envelopes and mail them. Within 60 days, you will receive at least $50,000 in cash.

NOTE: As soon as you mail out the letters, you are in the mail-order business. People will be sending you $2.00 to have their names placed on the mailing list along with the names of the others. This is a perfectly legal business transaction. More importantly, this is a way in which people are presently helping one another and have been for years. THAT is working within the system to make money without trying to justify selling something that no one needs or wants.

[The letter goes on to give a list of six names and addresses, followed by testimonials from participants.] Then—

"WHY DOES IT WORK SO WELL?"

Your receiving this letter is proof that it works. It works every time, but how well depends on how many letters you send out. In the example below, you mail out 200 letters. Imagine the money you'll receive if you mail 500. Here is how the system works. Assume, for example, you get a 7.5% rate of return, which is very conservative. My first attempt was about 9.5% and my second was 14.0%.

1. When you send 200 letters, 15 people will send you $2.00. $30.00
2. Those 15 mail out 200 letters and 225 people send you $2.00. $450.00
3. Those 225 mail out 200 letters and 3,375 people send you $2.00. $6,750.00
4. Those 3,375 mail out 200 letters and 50,625 people send you $2.00. $101,250.00
5. Those 50,625 mail out 200 letters and 759,375 send you $2.00. $1,518,750.00
At this point, your name leaves the list and you have received a <u>total</u> of: $1,627,230.00

Cost of Financial Freedom

Stamps (200)	$74.00
Envelopes	$3.00
Names/List	$35.00
Copies	$20.00
Originators (6)	$12.00
Total	$144.00

Not bad for Financial Freedom!!
If you don't try it, <u>you'll never know.</u>

REMEMBER FROM PAGE ONE, SHARE YOUR EARNINGS IN SOME GOOD WAY. <u>THAT IS WHAT MAKES THIS PROGRAM WORK!</u>

The sender neglected to observe that chain letters do not prompt people to produce anything of value. As in the case of gambling, money leaves many pockets, it ends up in a few pockets, and it does no good on the way. The letter writer argues that "it works," but so what? "It works" to run a casino too. Notwithstanding the sender's repeated denials, schemes such as this are definitely illegal, not to mention being definitely un-Christian.

Well, I've wasted enough of your time.

Expanding the Business

Recently an aviator's magazine made a rather surprising observation. A single-engine airplane is easier to land safely if its only engine fails than a twin-engine airplane is if one engine

> *"The bigger they come, the harder they fall."*

fails. That is correct; a twin-engine airplane running on one engine is harder to handle than a single-engine airplane with none.

Did you say, "Declare unto us this parable"? Well, sometimes a larger business looks more secure than a small one when it really is not. The owner of a big business has more money flowing through his hands, which can mean he has more resources to work with. But it can also mean he must beware of more snares, financial and spiritual.

Of course, businesses expand all the time and get away with it. One family living on a dirt road in the country hoped for a modest amount of growth when they moved their business to town. Actually, it more than doubled in the first year and grew from that point on.

But there are other stories too. A friend was making out all right as long as he operated his business in his garage. But then he thought of building a sizable shop out near the highway. He guessed correctly that the increased publicity would bring him more business. But he was wrong about the cost of building the shop.

> *Man explaining why his new shop was not bigger: "We figured it would be easier to make the place bigger if it was too small than to make the payments smaller if they were too big."*

Professional builders estimated the cost, but he could not believe it would cost that much and made his own estimate. Once the shop was built, he ended up making payments twice as large as he had expected. Finally he did the only sensible thing—he sold the shop. This put him almost back in the black, but it also put him out of the business.

Another friend expanded his farming operation and fell prey to the simplest and oldest of all disasters. During the night, his barn burned down. At least he got a good night's rest. No one realized what was happening until the next morning.

These are a few illustrations of what can happen. Especially beware of the trap of increased overhead. Just because your business is prospering in your garage does not mean it will prosper more if you move to town. You have to consider rent, the cost of city water, and the increased cost of electricity and telephone service (businesses pay higher rates than private homes do). Maybe you will be hiring an extra employee and will need to pay him wages.

Why should you expand at all? There might be good reasons.

—Maybe your children are growing up and need something to do.

—Maybe other people's children (or the parents themselves) need work to do.

—Maybe the demand for your product is increasing, and you do not want to let your customers down.

On the other hand, what are the alternatives to expanding your business?

—Send your children to work for someone else. Being obliged to work with other personalities than their own family will widen their world and give them a broader perspective of human nature.

—Help set someone else up in business. This hopefully will satisfy the increasing demand from your customers. And it will give someone the satisfaction of being in business for himself, not to mention your own satisfaction in helping to make that happen.

Always you need to consider the precedent you will set. If a number of brothers in the church are expanding, that gets a psychological snowball rolling that other business owners find hard to resist. The greatest pressure to expand does not come from the world but from the example of other businessmen in the church. The expansion mentality is not always healthy.

Remember too that if your business becomes quite big, you put yourself in a class along with professionals, with all the pitfalls that go along with that kind of life.

Finally, remember that God takes more than a casual interest in what is going on. He does not need our money, but He wants our love and loyalty, and He is more likely to get them if we have a business we can handle, financially and spiritually.

Two men were handling a large piece of furniture, one on one side and one on the other. One man had been in the moving business for many years, and he asked the other man a question that showed he knew his trade: "Do you have it, or does it have you?"

I trust you understand that parable.

Single-income Households

Many present-day families think that a single-income household is no longer possible. They say that supporting a family costs more than a working husband can provide. Mother must also earn to help meet the family's financial needs.

Yet, in their quiet, unassuming way, God-fearing families are showing that the world is wrong. Christian mothers happily serve at home. Faithful fathers adequately provide for the household. They prove that one income can still support a family.

Amazingly, this happens against many odds. We have larger families, refuse government handouts, give generously, and pay double for education (taxation and church offerings). What makes this possible?

1. *God's blessing.* This is a resource that the world does not have. Each day, we commit our needs to the One who has promised to supply all of them (Philippians 4:19). God honors our faith by strengthening our hands, reducing our needs, and pouring out His blessing.

2. *Bible direction.* God has outlined the place and responsibility of husband and wife. Father is the provider (I Timothy 5:8). Mother is a keeper at home (Titus 2:5), bearing children and guiding the house (I Timothy 5:14). Society's norm and economic pressures have not yet proved God's plan faulty or unworkable.

3. *Fulfillment in Christ.* Need levels are high in homes where Christ is rejected. These poor families try to fill the void with things that money can buy. But satisfaction cannot be bought, and though husband and wife both work, they "[earn] wages to put it into a bag with holes" (Haggai 1:6).

4. *Love at home.* This provides more than good home relationships; it affects family economics. Love lays the foundation for contentment at home and removes the appeal of restaurants, shopping malls, and recreational travel. Simplicity and sacrifice add to the joy in a loving Christian family.

5. *Mother's contribution.* "She . . . worketh willingly with her hands" (Proverbs 31:13), feeding, clothing, and caring for the family. She receives no formal paycheck, but knows how to compound the family's resources. As an effective "helper" in the family business, she adds to Father's earnings with her inspiration and helpful assistance. She spends little on herself and nothing at the hairdresser. Yet to God and the family, her worth and beauty are beyond compare.

6. *Christian economics.* Conservative money handling is part of our Mennonite heritage. We earn before we spend, and save before we borrow. Our family resources are not wasted on credit-card debts or installment payments for consumer goods. We view money as a stewardship trust from God.

7. *Help of the church.* The world's influence constantly strikes at our Biblical

lifestyle. No family can stand alone against this pressure. Every home needs the encouragement, example, and fellowship of a Scriptural church, which promotes and protects godly families.

Single-income households are not just relics of a past era in society. They stand as monuments of God's plan for the family. They show that a Biblical lifestyle, family integrity, and practical faith are still possible in the world today.[14]

3. Economizing

Defining Terms

What does the Bible tell us about saving money?

Well, that depends on what you mean by "saving." The Bible says little about *accumulating* money. In fact, it warns us against piling it up. "Your gold and silver is cankered; and the rust of them shall be a witness against you. . . . Ye have heaped treasure together for the last days" (James 5:3).

But the Bible does have something to say about *not wasting* money. We use the word *saving* for that too. In the process of not wasting money, we do accumulate some. Other parts of the book talk about that. In this part we want to think only about how not to waste it.

Not wasting our possessions is part of what we understand life to be all about. What other people do to "save the earth" or to "conserve resources," Christians do because it is the godly thing to do. "Gather up the fragments that remain," said Jesus, "that nothing be lost" (John 6:12). That was something symbolical as well as economical. Taking good care of what we have shows that we appreciate it. It is a roundabout way of saying "thank you" to God.

Leaving some things untouched in the first place is yet another way of showing our appreciation for God's providence. Consider King David's reaction after three soldiers risked their lives to bring him a drink of water from the well of Bethlehem. He poured it out! No, he was not ungrateful. Rather, his awe at what his men had done inspired his act. Maybe we should clarify that he poured it out "unto the LORD" (2 Samuel 23:16). Because of his gratitude, David did not grasp all the resources available

---

Simple and *economical* are not quite the same thing, even though this book uses them almost interchangeably. Living economically is only part of living simply. We live economically because it is good for our wallets. We live simply because it is good for *us*.

to him, and neither should we. Our lives should have the aura of being simply grateful and gratefully simple.

Not wasting money also needs some defining. The best buy for the money is not always the best buy for the soul. For example, God told the children of Israel to destroy the idols they came across in Palestine, and He warned them, "Thou shalt not desire the silver or gold that is on them" (Deuteronomy 7:25). No doubt some thrifty Israelites winced to see good gold and silver "go to waste." But that was the price of their spiritual safety. God did not want their souls to go to waste.

Achan hated to see a good garment and some gold and silver go to waste. So he helped himself. But a garment "hid in the earth" (Joshua 7:21) was not going to last long anyway, and the gold and silver did not seem to do him much good either.

In an incident of later Israelite history, King Amaziah paid a hundred talents of silver to hire an army from a neighboring nation to help him in a war against the Edomites. A prophet warned him that he was making a mistake and urged him to send the hired army home. Amaziah protested, "What shall we do for the hundred talents?" The prophet answered, "The LORD is able to give thee much more than this" (2 Chronicles 25:9).

One writer's comment is worth quoting here.

Sometimes we, like Amaziah, may get involved in situations that we had not anticipated. For example, we may become involved in a business that may seem good and right, but find later that the business is requiring too much time for our spiritual good. We may find that for the business to be financially successful we need to yoke up with unbelievers or in some way put ourselves into unwholesome company. Or we may find that we need to advertise with an appeal to the flesh or promote pleasure to sell our product. If the problem cannot be corrected, God is asking us to deliver ourselves from these involvements as soon as possible, at all costs. God is able to bless us far beyond what we will ever give up in material things.

We may also be faced with the question of what to do with clothing, shoes, or glasses that we are now aware are not consistent for us as Christians to wear. Should we wear them out, put them in the attic, or get rid of them? The answer may depend on the degree of objection, but we should not let the monetary value determine our decision. When the believers at Ephesus destroyed their objectionable possessions, the cost of them was fifty thousand pieces of silver (Acts 19:19).

Another example of monetary loss for the sake of principle would be in the area of cars. If we have bought a car that is objectionable, we must willingly spend the money to correct it, or else buy another one that will meet the Bible standard of separation and simplicity. It may involve selling the vehicle at a loss, but Christian principles must never be weighed in dollars and cents.[1]

Ways to Live Simply

It should be clear by now that living simply is not always simple. Besides, the standard varies somewhat from person to person. If we say, "Snowmobiles are wrong!" what will the rancher think who finds snowmobiles much more economical than horses? Still, we will put them on the list of things that conservative Christians raise their eyebrows about, because for many or most people the money could be used for better purposes. Here is the list.

Houses. A young man took a friend to his home. The friend had never seen it before, but when they pulled into a circle drive, he knew they were getting close. One of the houses along the drive looked quite pretentious, and the friend thought of teasing the driver about that house being his. It was a good thing he did not, because that was the house they pulled up to. It *was* his.

The inside of a house can be as telling as the outside. Kitchen installers shake their heads at the good cabinetry they must pull out of some people's houses so they can install something more to the owner's taste. And no doubt some homeowners shake their heads at *themselves* after they install a wood stove, only to realize that they are spending more to keep the stove going than they will ever save.

Jesus told us in Luke 14:13 to invite "the poor, the maimed, the lame, and the blind" into our homes. Is your house simple enough that when you do that, they will feel at ease?

Furniture. Someone came up with the following test questions on this issue.

—Is what others will think a consideration in your furniture buying?

—Do you feel the need of replacing furniture when it develops a used look?

—Does it mean something to you to have the right name on your furniture?

—Do you like to hear favorable comments on the quality of your furniture?

—Are you satisfied to buy used if that would fill the need from a practical standpoint?

—Do you discuss the poor selection of furniture in other homes?

—When establishing their own homes, do your children think in terms of simplicity and economy, or do they feel compelled to start with the new and the best?[2]

Clothes. A family was moving. The girls began bringing their dresses to the truck. Certain uncles who never missed a chance to chuckle had a good bit to say about the armloads the girls were bringing. Someone said, "MCC ought to be here!" (MCC is a relief organization.) The girls smiled, but maybe they were embarrassed too.

> *"Use it up,*
> *Wear it out,*
> *Make it do,*
> *Or do without."*

After asking yourself, "Is this garment appropriate for a Christian?" ask yourself one more question: "Do I need it?"

Food. The easiest way to waste food is to overeat. Company meals tend to invite this very thing. Food is for eating, right? Well, temptations are for resisting. If the hostess says, "Can't you eat more?" she is asking an irrelevant question. We do not eat until we can't eat more. Say, "I've had enough; thank you."

At home, save the leftovers. Certain beans, by popular consent, are better the second time around anyway. Lettuce salad is admittedly a different story, as it wilts pretty badly between meals, and no one considers putting it in soup or meat loaf.

Teach children to eat the apple down to the core. (A few people eat the core too!) The same principle applies to eating cantaloupe and watermelon.

Eat in rather than out. Why should you spend all that money

on installing a kitchen and then go eat in a restaurant?

When shopping for food, take a pocket calculator along. The cheapest calculators cost only a few dollars, and they can easily save you that much when you are looking for the best price per pound.

> *"Of the 8,000 products available in the average supermarket, only about 100 are good nutritional investments."*[3]

For basic good nutrition, shop the perimeter of the supermarket. There you will find vegetables, fruits, dairy products, eggs, meats, and so on. When walking the central aisles, keep a sharp eye on the top and bottom shelves. The middle shelves are often stocked with presweetened cereals and the like, at just the right level to catch the eyes of children. You might miss good values if you look only there.

Do not be too impressed with the word *natural* on labels. *Natural* has no legal definition.[4]

> *"I make the money first, and my wife makes it last."*

Go easy on the meat. It has been calculated that the calories in the beef from a steer are only one-thirtieth of the calories in the feed that the steer ate.[5] Of course, people eat meat for protein and maybe other benefits, not just for calories. Still, many people in the world survive nicely on beans and rice, or beans and corn, with relatively little meat. They get more protein for their money. For example, you can buy two pounds of bulk raw brown rice and half a pound of dried beans for less than it costs to buy a pound of hamburger, and you get twice as much protein.[6] When you do use meat, sometimes you can extend it by mixing it with other foods.

Remember to change with the times. Fish used to be called the poor man's meat. Not anymore! (Unless you are reading this fifty years after publication, and it is once more.) At the time of this writing, the cheapest meat is probably turkey or chicken.

Just a reminder: prices are higher at convenience stores than at a supermarket.

Coupons are often for things you do not want. Do not buy things just to get the value out of a coupon.

Conquer your fear of making economical dishes from recipes you never tried before. The first time is the worst. After that, you will feel much more comfortable.

> *"Never buy what you don't want, just because it's cheap."*

Kitchen equipment. Beware of single-purpose cookware. Will you really use a Crockpot all that much? If you will, fine. It will save you money. But it will not save you anything if you use it only once in two months. (If that one time is critically important, as when you have a fellowship meal, that is different.) The same principle applies to waffle irons, hamburger cookers, and popcorn poppers.

Invest most in the things you use every day. When the Smiths got married, Mrs. Smith's parents supplied her with high-quality pots and pans. She used them every day. Perhaps sixteen years later, the handle kept coming off one of the kettles. Mrs. Smith sent the kettle in to the company. They fixed it and sent a notice saying they wanted to inspect the other cookware too. So the Smiths piled everything in a box and sent it in. To their surprise, the company did not repair their cookware; they replaced it!

How could the company afford that? Well, the cookware was rather expensive in the first place, so the company did not go broke doing a favor. Besides, they believed (correctly) that the Smiths would tell their friends about this, which would encourage their friends to buy from the same company, and the company would soon make up for whatever they lost in replacing the cookware.

In addition, and this is the sad part, they knew that many people are poor managers. They do not wear out their kettles in a lifetime. They buy expensive new cookware and then eat out. Once again, if you do not intend to use a thing often, buy cheap or not at all. But if you intend to use it hard, buy quality if you can at all afford it.* That applies to anything from paintbrushes to used cars.

Pets. There is no such thing as a free pet. You have to feed it, to say the least. Then too, you might have to pay the veterinarian for some mishap or infection. Finally, in the case of a dog at least, the law might require you to put him to sleep gently when he gets old—again, for the cost of a doctor bill.

This is not to say that having a pet is always poor stewardship.

---

* Just remember that even "quality" can be overpriced to the point that it becomes a poor buy.

Many a dog has become a much-loved virtual member of the family for reasons that have little to do with money. I am just pointing out the financial side of it.

Having the more exotic pets can be poor management indeed. If you doubt that, check out some of the fancier fish in a large pet store. They can cost several hundred dollars apiece.

Vehicles. Owning a car might be the most expensive thing you ever do. If you are young, see how long you can put it off. Once you have finally bought a car, keep track of your expenses, comparing food, clothing, and lodging with car costs, and you will soon see what I mean.

It is not just the gas. It is not just the routine service jobs and tune-ups. It is the tires, brakes, tie rods, ball joints, hoses, water pumps, fuel pumps, alternators, mufflers, starters, and on and on. Then too, what about the cost of replacing the vehicle, and the taxes on the transfer? Again I say, put off buying a vehicle as long as you can.

Should you buy new or used? Some people buy new. They can order exactly what they want that way. On the other hand, the experts say things like this: "A new car loses nearly 25 percent of the price you pay for it the moment you drive it off the lot."[7] And again: "The quickest way to lose $2,000 is to drive a new car off the dealer's lot."[8] And again: "The cheapest car you will ever own is the car you have right now." A used-car ad sums it up this way: "Everyone drives a used car."

Remember, there might be the option of not having a car at all. City dwellers sometimes meet all their transportation needs by using buses, subways, and taxis. Some people bicycle to work, at least on sunny days.

When buying a vehicle, pay cash if you possibly can. Most of the cars you see on the road are not yet paid for. That means most car owners are paying much more for their cars than the figure they first saw on the price tag. Not only must they pay interest on their debt, but they miss the discount they might have gotten if they had paid cash.

Remember the old English proverb about being "penny wise and pound foolish." Do not buy a car just because it saves gas if the purchase will cost you more than you'll ever save on gas. One

> *"If you can't afford to save for a car, then you can't afford to borrow for it."[9]*

brother remarked, "Some people buy such expensive economy!" Of course, if you are buying a car anyway, you obviously should be concerned about the gas mileage.

Certain foreign cars are so costly to repair that the money you gain in fuel economy, you lose to the mechanic. Then too, some cars seem to need very frequent fixing. A repairman remarked years ago that FIAT (an Italian car) was an acronym for "Fix It Again, Tony!" Maybe he has changed his mind by this time. The point is, the reputation of a car is worth looking into before you buy it. You can find this information in books or magazines that give owners' reports on vehicles.

Once you have a good car, hang on to it. A friend remarked, "When I was young, I could hardly wait for my car to wear out so I could buy another one. Now I want my car to last as long as possible!"

Contentment is a wonderful thing. But remember that if you hang on to a car *too* long, you will start paying too many repair bills. At some point, it becomes more economical to buy something newer and more dependable.

Travel. We cannot always just stay home. Sometimes spending good money to visit and encourage good people is better stewardship than not spending it.

But we should *sometimes* choose to stay at home. We should not be bitten by the wanderlust bug, neither should we visit all the good places we can think of to go.

What is more, we can be economical when we travel. A good time to practice this precept is on school trips. One father gave his children money for school trips but told them that what they saved they could keep. This dampened the souvenir buying considerably because the children wanted the greater satisfaction of bringing their money home again.

Taking in some scenic attractions as we travel might have a place. But we need to be choosy. A highly advertised attraction might be expensive, and a high entrance fee might be just the beginning of sorrows if the attraction turns out to have unsavory features. But waterfalls, forests, historical attractions, and places of business (like shipyards) are less likely to be disappointing.

Gadgets and accessories. We make butter out of cream. Someone said he came across a gadget for making cream out of butter! That sounds like the height of folly! Nonetheless, some folks quickly fall for foolish, unnecessary gadgets.

Can you be satisfied with a camera that fits your actual needs? Catalogs and salesmen do their best to dazzle customers into buying more and more complex cameras—with proportionate price tags, of course. Somewhere you have to draw the line, even if a friend of yours draws his line a hundred dollars higher.

Think twice before buying a computer. Will a pocket calculator do? A computer saves time when doing big jobs, but it can waste time when doing small ones.

Telephone. Keep a sharp eye on those phone bills. These days you can call across the country for just pennies a minute. This makes it economical to phone instead of to write. Indeed, there are old friends and loved ones you *should* call, perhaps more often than you do. But

> *"Buy that thou hast no need of, and ere long thou shalt sell thy necessities."[10]*

somehow the pennies add up faster than you think. If you must call a friend who does not know when to hang up, call five minutes before you must rush out the door for an appointment, or just before someone else in the family must use the phone. Then you can explain that you do not have much time to talk.

By the way, there are still times to write or send cards instead of calling. Your loved ones cannot set pretty phone calls on the windowsill or reread them from time to time.

Recreation. Do good Christians believe in any form of recreation? They certainly do, but it is just not the kind that the world talks about. Good recreation re-creates the body, mind, or spirit—usually all three. And it does not cost so much that you need still more recreation after you have paid off the costs of the recreation.

Take some of your breaks on the run. "A change is as good as a rest." If you have been exercising your muscles all day, it feels good to take a break from that and read a book on the back porch. If you have been studying all day, it feels good to go out and cut wood for a while. You do not have to do something unproductive in order to call it recreation.

Discover recreation that is already beckoning. You probably have a field guide to wildflowers or birds or butterflies somewhere on your bookshelf. Rediscover a book or two.

Recreation is often more interesting with children. Try taking a child through a museum and explaining things as you go, rather than wandering through it all by your lonesome or even with other adults. At home, put up a tire swing or hammer together a pair of stilts. In the evening, let a child sit on your lap for a story. Count it a priceless moment. Many people would give a good bit for that privilege.

> *"Be content with such things as ye have" (Hebrews 13:5).*

Walk past the recreational vehicle store with a smile. Someone asked a friend if he spends quite a bit on his children's Christian education. The friend replied, "I'd guess you spend just as much as that on your snowmobile and all that goes with it." The questioner said, "No!" But after a bit of thought, he admitted that it might be true. Make your own application. Boats . . . off-road vehicles . . . campers . . . they can cost more than you ever expected.

Use "armstrong equipment" as much as possible. That is a pun, of course. Do you really need a snowblower in your shed when you have a pair of *strong arms* that can clear the driveway almost as fast as a snowblower and can grow stronger by the experience?

Give hunting the acid test. Some people object to hunting for reasons other than stewardship, but we are talking only about stewardship now. Granted—hunting might pay if we keep it local, but that becomes pretty iffy if we must drive all the way to Deer County to do it. Having an expensive gun collection, with all the other paraphernalia that hunters collect, gets pretty questionable too. We should consider the image we give to people around us, whether they see us in the forest or see a gun cabinet at home.

Gifts. Friends of ours found a sensible way to wrap a wedding gift—they used a towel. I am confident the towel did not end up crumpled in the trash can.

As for pre-wedding gift showers, don't the bride and groom get enough at wedding time?

Small items. Do not nickel-and-dime yourself to death.

Beware the advertisements that ignore this concept. So that kerosene heater costs only pennies a day? How *many* pennies? Multiply it by thirty: how much is that per month?

A small teddy bear to hang from your car mirror might not cost much. But how many other nickels and dimes (and dollars) are you spending here and there?

"Teach your dollars more cents."

Simple carelessness can cheat you. A whole house lit up for two people might be a sign that the two people are careless in some other ways too.

Impulse buying. Stick to your shopping list, and do not shop for groceries when you are hungry, as you will tend to buy more.

Learn the fine art of procrastination! Look at what the first ballpoint pens cost. Look at the first pocket calculators. Not only will the price drop in the future, there will also be fewer problems with the product. Maybe you will decide you do not even need it.

On the same principle, try waiting to buy strawberries for a few weeks after the strawberry season has begun. See if you can wait to buy that new kerosene heater until just after Christmas.

Medical bills. We can help each other rather than looking to insurance. But we can fall into the same trap others do if we assume that no matter what medical problems we have, someone will pay the bill. That is not fair.

We can save on medical bills by keeping ourselves healthy. We do not simply have to hope the lightning will not strike. "Diseases of choice" are the kind we do not need to have if we take care of ourselves. Of course, drinking and smoking are not a problem among most readers, which is more of a medical blessing than we often realize.

"You don't have to brush and floss all your teeth, just the ones you want to keep."

Other lifestyle problems are harder to avoid. We cannot simply quit eating; therefore, at every meal we have to use our judgment. We can pass up the second piece of shoofly pie. We can go easy on the salt and cream and sugar. We can develop a taste for lettuce salad, maybe garnished with raisins and sunflower seeds. There are all kinds of possibilities, including some that ruin the purpose of the salad.

We can pay a certain amount of attention to physical fitness. Going for regular walks will help to improve our outlook, it makes us better workers, and it works as well as or better than vitamins. The price is right too. In fact, getting regular exercise might even save time. I can't believe how people who never find time to take care of themselves always find time to go to the doctor.

We can try to see the problems of life as challenges rather than frustrations. Many illnesses start with mental stress. People who do not believe in smoking can still hurt themselves by fuming.

Some years ago a study was made of a group of Italians living in a small town in Pennsylvania. Though they tended to eat heartily and gain weight, they had little heart disease. But if one of them moved to the city, he fell subject to the same heart problems that other people had. Lack of stress in the small town and a cheerful attitude toward life seemed to make the difference.[11]

Of course, in ancient times it was written, "Let the peace of God rule in your hearts, . . . and be ye thankful" (Colossians 3:15). This is as good as a medical prescription.

Around the house. Learn how to do the simpler jobs. You need not call the plumber to fix a leaky faucet. Admittedly, I ended up buying a new faucet the last time I tried, but the experience did me good.

Fix scratches in furniture with crayon. It's effective, it's rather fun, and it's what furniture dealers do anyway.

Remember the simple upkeep jobs. If the oil in the lawn mower runs out and you ruin the engine, that is not just a loss but an embarrassment. Christians should not do things like that!

Repair your own car when you can. Many mechanical jobs are well within the range of a can-do young fellow, even if all he has is a cheap socket set. He can get parts from a parts store downtown, just as professionals do. If he gets stuck partway through the job, he can probably call a friend for a little advice.

Of course, sometimes a car repair is beyond your ability. No doubt every professional repairman can tell stories about towing in the car of some crestfallen backyard mechanic. Oh, well, that is the risk you take.

Avoid paying hundreds of dollars for equipment you can rent. If you use a pressure washer only once every year or two, rent one. You will not feel the thrill of acquisition, but you will not feel the burden of it either.

Avoid renting what you can borrow. Friends might actually take it as a compliment that you thought of borrowing from them. (Wouldn't you have felt complimented if you had owned the donkey Jesus borrowed to ride into Jerusalem?) Just remember to return the item promptly, with the gas tank refilled if it has a gas tank, and do your friends a favor sometime. Everyone says this is the kind of thing people did a hundred years ago, and they wish we would do more of it. Well, at least we can start.

Try cutting your boys' hair—and your own too, if you are Father. The main thing to remember is that you can always take more off if you have not taken enough off, so take it a little easy. For your first few tries, rather than trying to fix your errors, brush yourself off and go to your former barber and let him touch you up. You will catch on after a few times.

Remember to teach these habits to your children too. You will multiply your good influence if you do, and you will regret it if you do not. The daughter who leaves home not knowing how to sew has been cheated.

The tax benefits of living savingly. Paying taxes is part of being a good citizen. But even the government approves of your managing in such a way as not to pay more taxes than you have to. Wasn't it Benjamin Franklin who said, "A penny saved is a penny earned"? If he lived today, he might add, "And you do not have to pay income tax on it."

For calculation purposes, suppose we call that penny a dollar. If you earn a dollar, you will have to pay twenty cents or more of that for income tax, so all you will have left is eighty cents at best. But if you save a dollar by economizing, it is all yours.

We will take this concept a step further. To buy an $80 stepladder, you need to earn $100, assuming that only eighty cents of each dollar is yours after taxes (80% of $100 = $80). If you can find a decent used stepladder for $50, you need to earn

79

only $62.50. You thought you saved $30 by buying the $50 ladder, but you actually saved $37.50—the difference between what you would have needed to earn in one case as compared with the other.

We could go even further and talk about what your money could earn you if you put it in the bank, but we will wait to discuss that until Chapter 4.

Personal satisfactions of living simply. It is said that Diogenes, the ancient Greek philosopher, lived so simply that he reduced his possessions to a simple bowl. He carried it around and put into it the food that people gave him. One day Diogenes tripped and broke his bowl. What do you think he said? "I'm free!"

> *"It is harder to carry a full cup than an empty one."*[12]

Most of us have not taken simplicity quite to that extent, but somehow the story strikes a chord in us. We recognize the light feeling that comes when we have unloaded. What does the Bible say? "The sleep of a labouring man is sweet, whether he eat little or much: but the abundance of the rich will not suffer him to sleep" (Ecclesiastes 5:12).

Then too, there is the satisfaction of posing problems for ourselves and figuring them out. "How can I do this most simply?" we ask ourselves; and after we have learned a good way, we take pleasure in the discovery. Someone remarked, "About half the time when people ask me what's the reason for simple living, I say, 'It's more fun.' "[13]

Living simply creates a bond with other people who are also living simply. Most of us do not altogether follow the example of the believers in Acts 2, who "had all things common." But we certainly concede that having all things common gave them a brotherly feeling and a common denominator.

Another benefit of living simply is that "toughing it out" can make us a little tougher spiritually. "He that hath suffered in the flesh hath ceased from sin" (1 Peter 4:1). A soft, luxurious life can make us soft spiritually.

Sometimes we do without a blessing for a while and are rewarded by later getting it back in greater measure. During a storm, one man used to step outside his door to feel the chill and see the fury of the wind and rain. Then he would step back into his house and enjoy how snug and cozy it was inside.

"Hunger is the best sauce," and the only way to get that sauce is to go hungry for a little while. I do not have much time for

> *"Pleasure's couch is virtue's grave."*[14]

people who go without breakfast so they can stuff themselves at the smorgasbord come lunchtime. But I do respect people who fast for other reasons. One of their incidental rewards is enjoying their food a little more once they start eating again.

Putting off getting some new possession is a way of doing the same thing, be it a pickup, a dog, or a sweater. Of course there comes a time to say "Now," but that moment will be sweeter if we have not said it too soon.

You can do without almost anything if you know you may have it again sometime. And some things you can put off indefinitely if you know you can have them in the world to come. We talk about the "stranger and pilgrim concept," which is another way of saying the same thing.

A traveler once visited a home so sparsely furnished that he asked the man of the house, "Where's your furniture?"

The man of the house replied, "Where's yours?"

"I don't have any," said the traveler. "I'm just passing through."

"So am I."[15]

Finding Bargains

Bargains make some people's eyes glow. It is almost a game with them. A bright orange sticker marked "$2 off" makes them want to buy, even if the price is the same on another box with no sticker. Stores on back streets hold more appeal to them than glistening supermarkets, and discovering a pair of shoes hanging by its strings at a farmers' market thrills them more than getting a perfect fit at one of the shoe stores in the mall. Sometimes even fashionable folks get bargain fever and poke around at flea markets, surplus stores, and Ye Olde Junque Shoppe.

Actually, none of us are totally immune to the thrill of a good deal. This is not altogether bad, but it makes us vulnerable to certain traps. Often we tend to be shortsighted when a bargain presents itself.

What is cheap might turn out not to be economical. An unmarried young man bought a used couch with a bit of a sag in the seat, but he thought little of it. When his mother saw it, she began reminiscing about their earlier housekeeping days. She said, "We bought furniture that didn't look too bad, but it wasn't long before it did look bad." Cheap, yes. Economical, no.

> *"The bitterness of poor quality lasts long after the sweetness of low price is forgotten."*

What is cheap might be too far away to be worth the hassle. Do not drive five miles to save fifty cents. Suppose the Arco station out near the freeway offers gas at four cents less than the Chevron station downtown. Going to Arco involves a round trip of ten miles. If your car gets twenty miles to the gallon, how much will you pay for the half gallon it takes to get to the Arco station and back? If you put as much as twenty gallons in your car at this fill-up, saving four cents a gallon, you will save eighty cents. But how much will you have lost, considering the wear and tear on your car and saying nothing of your time?

That does not mean you should never shop around. Suppose the NAPA store in town sells three-gallon gas cans for $17.00, Jones Lumber sells them for $8.50, and a discount center near another town sells them for $6.00. You would not want to run to the discount center just for that one purchase, but you would surely want to buy it there if you need to go for some other reason.

But even at the bargain counter, things will not always be bargains. People tell stories of fancy glass bottles offered for sale at higher prices than the bottles would have cost new—and full! Some people buy items for $2.50 at public sales and feel good

---

It seems that a bright young salesman was trying to sell a new dishwasher to a housewife. "Madam," he said, "if you buy this dishwasher, it will save you the cost of a maid. You will be saving every month."

The housewife hesitated. "Well, I am not sure we can buy it. We bought a car to save bus fare. Then we bought a television to save movie expense. Last week we bought a clothes washer to save laundry bills. You know, mister, I think we are already saving so much that we can't afford to save any more."[16]

until they learn that they could have bought the same thing for $1.98 in the store. Storekeepers themselves sometimes offer big bags of certain items, say sugar, at higher prices per pound than smaller ones, contrary to what customers expect—yes, and sell them.* Slogans like "Compare and save!!" sound great, but did the customer compare? Maybe he did not save as much as he thought.

Public auctions can be especially treacherous to the unwary or excitable. The classical auctioneer (they vary, of course) knows how to get people's blood stirring, first with his humorous comments and then with his way of making bidders feel like heroes as long as they keep bidding. If you are the kind that gets carried away, and even if you are not, you had better set a price in your mind, bid confidently up to that figure, and then shake your head.

Always be mindful of the language in which a thing is presented. Millions of customers have eaten with zest the famous hamburgers called quarter-pounders, but how many people would

> *"A rose by any other name would smell as sweet,"* but most of us don't act as if we believe it.

have bought them had they been called four-ouncers? Uncle Isaac once saw on a restaurant menu an item called a "tube steak." Curious, he ordered the tube steak—and got a hot dog.

In all our eagerness to be nobody's fool, however, let us remember courtesy. Some business owners dread to see certain people walk in, because those customers want to haggle for everything. Individuals known for their religious lifestyle can be among the worst. Let us not be so aggressive in driving bargains that we spoil an otherwise good testimony. "Thou shalt love thy neighbour as thyself" must govern all that a Christian does, even when he is looking for bargains. After all, we are not here to acquire things but to win people so that we can finally enjoy them forever in the presence of the Lord.

---

* The storekeeper is not necessarily trying to deceive his customers. He can offer 5-pound bags of sugar at a lower price per pound because they move faster than 25-pound bags.

Avoiding Checking-account Traps

The average holder of a checking account, we are told, bounces six checks a year. If he has to pay twenty dollars in penalties every time, that is quite a bit of money.

Furthermore, if he has one of those automated agreements in which the bank pays his bills out of his account for him, he runs into trouble if the money is not there. Every business day after his account runs short, the creditors that did not get their money yesterday come back to the bank looking for their money again. Every business day, each of them charges another penalty of twenty dollars or so. Slap. Slap. Slap. Meanwhile, the bank treats each of those episodes like a bounced check, charging a penalty for every business day his account runs short—so he gets two slaps a day!

> *Do you really have time to sit down and write out a bunch of checks each month? See how easy online billing and payment can be. Free.*
>
> *—Puget Sound Energy flyer*

However, one can deliver himself from this if he gets the bank to stop his automated payments.

George ran his checking account skimmingly low, but he did his arithmetic carefully and knew he had six dollars left in the bank. He was startled when the bank informed him that two of his checks had bounced and that his account now stood at fifty-two dollars in the red. What had gone wrong?

George had forgotten that whenever he ran his account below a hundred dollars, the bank charged a fee of eight dollars. This put him into the red by two dollars. Then the bank charged him twenty dollars for being in the red, putting him at twenty-two below. Later, not realizing what had happened, George deposited a hundred dollars and promptly wrote out several checks totaling ninety dollars, thinking he had sixteen dollars to spare. The fact is, the hundred dollars had only brought his balance up to seventy-eight dollars. His first check, for eighty dollars, took the balance below zero again. So the checks bounced, and the bank charged him $20 on each bounced check.

Grandpa keeps a little poster in his garage that says, "How can I be overdrawn? I still have checks!" This is supposed to be obviously and instantly funny to the reader. But the fact that

Uncle Raymond does not quite comprehend this is not so funny. When he writes out a check for ninety-seven dollars, he does not understand that the ninety-seven dollars is gone. If a bank statement arrives the next day assuring him that the money is still there, that is good enough for him. Poor Uncle Raymond. He never will understand outstanding checks, which is one reason why someone else has to help him manage his money.

Dealing With Financial Loss

Losses hurt. They are so uneconomical. All that we scraped together and saved disappears in a twinkling. Indeed, losses seem sacrilegious. They seem to destroy our efforts to honor the Lord by carefully managing the gifts He has given us.

A loss does not stop with the loss itself. We feel stung by what it represents—the loss of independence, the feeling that we do not know what will happen next, that things are out of our control.

Finally, we often suspect that the loss served us right somehow. Maybe we should have managed better. Maybe we were too greedy and lost by grasping too much. Maybe we were not thankful enough for what we did have.

Yet loss—even disaster—is not the end of the world. Some people try too hard to avoid facing losses. For example, they might try to work out their own financial salvation by going bankrupt. Once they have done this, their creditors have to be satisfied with whatever fraction of the pie they can get. In fact, some people go to inordinate lengths to avoid loss before it ever comes. Some are so well insured that to all appearances the Lord cannot touch their possessions.

The wisest people are prudent enough to avoid most losses but big enough not to go to pieces if they come. An elderly farmer watched his barn flaming against the night sky for a while; then he said to the fire chief, "I'll think I'll go now and get some sleep." The chief looked doubtfully at one of the farmer's sons, and the son said, "He probably will!"

> *"If you can meet with triumph and disaster / And treat those two impostors just the same . . ."*[17]

Not every Christian would be quite so calm at such a time, for personalities vary. But every one should be able to "hear a little music in the background," even in the worst of situations. The apostle Paul would have said, "I know both how to be abased, and I know how to abound: every where and in all things I am instructed both to be full and to be hungry, both to abound and to suffer need" (Philippians 4:12).

Why is financial disaster not the end of the world?

Losers have good company. The patriarch Isaac lost his wells when he backed away from them to make peace with his neighbors. Job, of course, lost everything he had. Down through history, people have lost homes and businesses because of religious persecution. And most of us can point to good people around us who lost a considerable amount for one reason or another. One brother took a financial beating when he moved to a mission field. Another brother's new house was ransacked from top to bottom, and all his carpentry tools were stolen. In none of these cases did loss come because the owner was in the wrong.

Losses can be educational. Sometimes it is the little losses that get us—the garment that turns out to be too small but cannot be returned, the crumpled fender, the flashlight left on over the weekend. But maybe the little losses give us opportunities to learn from small mistakes instead of having to learn from big ones.

Recently some boys wanted to buy insulated wire. They found wire for about sixty dollars but thought that was pretty expensive. So they went to another store and found another kind of wire for maybe ten dollars less. It was not what the manual called for, but the man at the store thought it would probably work. It did not; and instead of saving ten dollars, the boys found themselves out of pocket in the amount of some fifty dollars.

They took it well. Their father told them that learning a lesson on sixty dollars might save them quite a few thousand dollars sometime. In the end, the boys figured out a way to salvage their purchase, and it was not lost after all. So they learned two lessons—how not to do it wrong, and how to make do after they had done it wrong.

Even if God allows us a major disaster, that is no cause for utter despair. The Old Testament Israelites suffered some severe calamities, but always God had a prophet on hand to say, in effect, "Learn from this! Do better in the future!"

> "Stumbling blocks can sometimes be made into steppingstones."

And God was always disappointed if they did not. "The people turneth not unto him that smiteth them," He once lamented (Isaiah 9:13). But God was pleased when the Israelites broke the negative pattern in the days of Haggai. This prophet pointed out that they were suffering losses because they had been putting their interests ahead of God's. "He that earneth wages earneth wages to put it into a bag with holes" (Haggai 1:6). After the people changed, God declared, "From this day will I bless you" (Haggai 2:19). Their losses had been educational.

Losses teach us who is in charge of our lives. The more we hurt at losing control of our lives, the more we have reason to suspect that we loved control too much. King David learned this lesson after he numbered his armies to find out how many men were under his control. God responded, in effect, "David, I'll give you some control. Choose one of three disasters: famine, military defeat, or pestilence." Which do you want, King David—chocolate, vanilla, or strawberry? Seeing who really was in charge of his life, David responded, "Let me fall now into the hand of the LORD." (See 1 Chronicles 21:9–13).

Losses in themselves are not wrong. God may have purposes in them that we know nothing about. He certainly did in the case of Job. It is not clear even to this day whether Job ever found out about the conversations between God and Satan, in chapters 1 and 2. When God spoke to Job out of the whirlwind at the close of the story, it was only to impress on Job how little he knew and how little he needed to know. Just to be faithful in disaster was all that was necessary.

> Sometimes a child of God has more in his pocket, sometimes less. But he is as rich one day as the next. Whether he receives a legacy or gets a doctor bill does not change what he has in the bank of heaven.

Stephen did not know all of God's purposes when he lost his life (Acts 7). Yet he could see Jesus standing at the right hand of God to welcome him, and he was content. God used Stephen's loss to serve His own purposes. And God uses

> *"If any man will sue thee at the law, and take away thy coat, let him have thy cloke also" (Matthew 5:40).*

our financial losses, too—sometimes to draw us closer to Himself, sometimes to draw other people closer.

Finally, losses hurt because we have the idea that the more resources we have, the better we can serve the Lord. That is not true. God does not need our resources. He needs us.

In some ways, our handling of finances and possessions is like a board game with play money and pretend properties. The game is exciting, but suddenly it is over, the board is folded up, and the players move on to the real world. There were no real gains and no real losses. The only real value in the game was in whatever skills or virtues the players may have gained as they played it.

The money we handle on earth is not play money, yet there are similarities. Our real riches are not here; they are elsewhere. Suddenly it will all be over, and the Lord will evaluate not how much we have gained or lost monetarily, but how well and faithfully we have served Him. On that basis He will commit to our trust the true riches (Luke 16:11).

To be practical, we must face the fact that we need possessions here. God expects us to take good care of them. But in the final analysis, all earthly losses are acceptable. The Lord is well able to make them up to us in the world to come. "Ye . . . took joyfully the spoiling of your goods, knowing in yourselves that ye have in heaven a better and an enduring substance" (Hebrews 10:34).

We can afford to lose. We are children of the King.

Practical Advice About Cutting One's Losses

Cutting your losses means giving up the effort of trying to salvage your money's worth from a project or property. You will lose by putting it behind you, but you will also stop losing.

Know when to sell. Andrew got a phone call from his mechanic. His car was on the lift, and the mechanic wanted to make sure he really wanted to pay the money it would take to get it fixed.

Andrew said, "Can I call you back in five minutes?" After a word with the Lord, he called and said, "Take it off the lift. I'll try to sell it for a mechanic's special."

The mechanic said, "We were talking about it here in the shop, and we were thinking the same thing."

The next vehicle Andrew bought was a van for $1,600. Someone remarked, "For that kind of money, you could drive it for ten thousand miles and then push it over a cliff, and it wouldn't owe you anything." Sometime later, Andrew remarked, tongue-in-cheek, "Now I wish I had." The van served him well for a time, but then the transmission had to be rebuilt, and there were many other repairs. The engine took a great deal of oil. The proprietor of the corner store started keeping larger containers of oil in stock. "I bought it with you in mind," he said.

Finally the engine lost its oil pressure, and Andrew had to do something in a hurry—either have the engine rebuilt (and keep on repairing the rest of the van) or buy a newer vehicle. At that point he bought a newer van that served him well for many years.

By the way, is it fair to sell someone a car you yourself would not buy? Yes, if you tell him frankly about your vehicle's flaws and sell it to him for a decent price. If he is mechanically inclined or has a brother-in-law who does not mind fixing it up for a song, he might make out better with the vehicle than you would if you kept it.

Do not throw good money after bad. Do not think, "I've already put this much money into it. If I get rid of it now, all that money will be lost. The only way I can save it is to fix it again, and hopefully, this will be the last repair!" Sometimes that is true, but usually it is not. Cut your losses, and forget about it.

The Miller family had a man come out and fix their dryer so many times that the Miller children started calling him "the dryer man." They finally got another dryer. If they had known they were going to buy a dryer anyway, they could have bought it earlier and saved money.

Of course, you hear the other kind of story too. Grandpa had a car that no longer ran. He decided it was funeral time and called Mr. Dull (his actual name), the junkyard man. Grandpa asked what the junkyard would give for a car like his. Mr. Dull answered, "People bring them here and let them sit!" Finally Grandpa had the car towed to the junkyard.

Later someone told him that a man at the junkyard had figured out what was wrong with the car and fixed it. "It runs like a top!" the person said. So you see, we sometimes make errors in judgment despite our best intentions. These things help to keep us humble.

A Useful Word

Mr. Zeller, the insurance man, once taught young Jonathan a useful word without meaning to. Jonathan's father had left him with Mr. Zeller to sign up for liability insurance. Mr. Zeller was very pleasant and agreed to work with what Jonathan wanted. Then he said, "Now there's another kind of insurance . . ." And he explained the benefits of comprehensive insurance. "This," he said, "covers damage that might happen to your car even if you do not have a collision. Maybe a pheasant flies into your grill, or a stone hits your windshield."

Jonathan did not want the insurance. So he tried to give reasons why he preferred not to have it. But every time he came up with a reason not to have it, Mr. Zeller kindly gave him a reason why he should. Finally, because he could not argue the man down, Jonathan bought the insurance.

It occurred to him later that he would not have had to. All he would have had to say was "No." That is a simple, unassailable word. As the popular saying goes, "What part of *no* don't you understand?"

To be polite, Jonathan could have surrounded the *no* with a few extra words. "No, thank you, I'm not interested" would have gotten the point across.

Incidentally, the words *not interested* mean the same as *no* and are generally taken that way. If a telemarketer asks you to switch your long-distance carrier and you do not want to, you need not bother saying something lame, such as "I like my present phone company pretty well." The telemarketer will say, "I understand, but . . ." and keep right on talking. You have to say, "Thanks, but I'm not interested!" as early in the conversation as you can get a word in edgewise. Interrupt if you have to. It sounds crusty; but if you do not do it, you will waste time and risk having another telemarketer from the same company call you again next Tuesday.

Insurance

Insurance is a systematic way to share losses so that everyone can hurt a little and no one has to hurt too much. It is a secular way of doing what the Christian church is designed to do. The apostle Paul put it like this: "For I mean not that other men be eased, and ye burdened: but by an equality, that now at this time your abundance may be a supply for their want, that their abundance also may be a supply for your want: that there may be equality" (2 Corinthians 8:13, 14).

There are different kinds of insurance, such as auto insurance, fire insurance, life insurance, medical insurance, and workmen's compensation. And there are different kinds of kinds. For example, auto insurance may involve comprehensive insurance, collision insurance, and liability insurance. In most cases, the insured person makes regular payments, called premiums, to the insurance company; and as long as he pays, the company agrees to protect him in case of a loss. He can choose to get a higher percentage of his loss covered if he likes, in which case he will pay higher premiums.

To anyone who faces a loss, the advantages offered by insurance are obvious. If he lands in the hospital with a broken back, medical insurance will cover his bills. If he spends a long time at home convalescing, workmen's compensation may help. If he dies, life insurance will cover his funeral bills and give his family something to help them through the lean times ahead.

However, there are several arguments against insurance for Christians.

Insurance makes God's people disinclined to take care of their own. We ought to be helping each other because it draws us together. True, insurance is also a way of helping other people, but insurance does not draw people together. It excludes unhealthy people because they are considered poor risks. It excludes poor people because they cannot afford to pay premiums. Even people who have insurance look at insurance more as a business than as a brotherhood. Insurance robs church people of the privilege of helping each other and appreciating each other the more because of it.

Insurance militates against faith in God. Even those Christians who promote insurance admit that there is such a thing as too much insurance.

The way of faith is to trust in the Lord to provide for the uncertainties of life. And He provides especially through His people. Middle-aged parents have died, and their widowed mates have gone on with life, receiving help from their brothers and sisters in the family and in the church. Sometimes that help has taken the form of a boost in starting a business so that the widowed father or mother could work at home and be with the children.

Insurance plays on fear. Insurance agents say things like, "All you have to do is collide with a busload of schoolchildren, and you will face enough lawsuits to ruin you." But the suppositions can go on and on. All you have to do is be run over by a busload of schoolchildren, and you will die!

Insurance does not consider God. It does not consider angels. All it considers is probability tables. True, the laws of probability were created by God; but finally, God remains the master of it all. He does not simply sit back and watch His natural laws work.

"We know that all things work together for good to them that love God, to them who are the called according to his purpose" (Romans 8:28).

Insured people do not get a good return on their premiums. For every dollar they pay to insurance companies, how much help do they get in return when they have an illness or an accident? The average is a few dimes.[18] The rest of the dollar is used up for advertising, overhead, and of course, profit for the insurance companies.

Since we like to economize, why not economize here? Rather than taking out insurance, we would be better off saving our money and helping each other through the church when necessary. Our deacons do their work without dipping into the money they collect. Virtually every dollar placed in the offering goes to a person who needs it.

Insurance encourages lawsuits and high fees. Patients sue doctors because they know that their doctors are insured and can produce money. Doctors, in turn, charge high rates of their patients because they know their patients are insured and can produce money!

Even the insurance folks are uneasy about the vicious cycle. An ad once pictured a courtroom, with a caption that ran something like this: "The jury smiled when they awarded an accident victim $100,000. They didn't know it was coming out of their own pockets. . . . No one likes higher premiums. But we're telling it straight."

Insurance encourages carelessness. An insurance advertisement proclaimed, "Without insurance, your life would be a deathtrap." True, insurance companies require people to get rid of certain hazards before they insure them. But insurance companies create as many problems as they solve. Brother John was called to bring his wrecker to the scene of a truck accident. The trailer was partly tipped and in danger of tipping over completely, causing considerable loss. He told the police that to avoid further damage, another wrecker should be called. With careful work, the trailer could be saved. An officer responded, "It's insured, isn't it?" Brother John was dismissed. Presumably the police called out some other wrecker that did it the easy way.

Insurance companies tempt otherwise honest people to cheat.
One writer put it well: "People whom you could trust with your
wallet will cheat their insurance companies without compunction.
Doctors and mechanics inflate bills. People make false claims
and inflate rightful ones. Others have murdered to collect life
insurance benefits. And it is a fact that small business fires
increase during recessions."[19]

> While Daddy lives,
> He does his best.
> If Daddy dies,
> God does the rest.[20]

*Insurance companies will avoid paying
claims if possible.* A brother was involved in
an accident. He made the mistake of saying
in front of the insurance adjuster, "I didn't
think the other driver would do what he
did." The insurance man replied, "You weren't supposed to think
that." The brother learned too late to watch his words around
an insurance adjuster because insurance companies will use the
smallest excuse to avoid paying. (In this case, "I didn't think" was
taken as admission of fault.) Often people have to sue before an
insurance company will pay up. Even then they might go away
empty-handed if the company can prove that some item in the
fine print lets them off.

No doubt some of your friends can tell stories of their own.
A friend of the writer went to the hospital to have a procedure
done. The hospital had already prepared her for the procedure
when it became evident that the insurance company was not
going to pay. The hospital let her go home without doing the
procedure. Someone at the hospital remarked, "You have the
wrong insurance company."

It is much more heartwarming and dependable to look to the
Lord and His people, not hoping the insurance policy will have
no escape clause but trusting in Him who is a "very present help
in trouble." "A Scriptural brotherhood assistance program is far
superior to any earthly life insurance program. Its participants
are involved not because of what they can get out of it but rather
because of a love for the brethren and a desire to share in their
burdens. It provides for needy persons regardless of their abilities
or their previous contributions. It does not turn away any because
they are no longer able to pay their insurance premiums. It does
not have a monetary profit motive, but rather it is a plan that

will profit all participants spiritually, whether they are giving or are receiving."[21]

What about 1 Timothy 5:8? It says, "But if any provide not for his own, and specially for those of his own house, he hath denied the faith, and is worse than an infidel." In light of this, one respected financial planner favors life insurance for a father "if his church, or other members of his family do not have the desire or ability to provide for a young family. . . . Life insurance, however, does not eliminate the responsibility of the church to care for its own. Unfortunately, as we have become more mobile in our society and have fewer close relationships, the church itself does not feel the burden of caring for those in its midst who have a legitimate need."[22] He is not describing your church, is he? Most readers of this book have all the resources in their church that many people wish for.

One caution: churches are churches, not insurance companies. The New Testament specifies that individuals and their families are responsible for their own financial affairs but that the church is to help as necessary (1 Timothy 5:3, 4). It is better to wait for the deacon to knock on our door when we have a financial problem,

Mrs. Carter found a lump on her neck, so she went to Dr. Dunn. When he learned that the Carters did not have insurance, he trimmed what would normally have been a bill of one hundred dollars to thirty dollars. He referred her to a specialist, Dr. Matlock.

When Dr. Matlock heard that they did not have insurance, he wondered if the Carters would have a problem with paying the bill for the day's visit. Maybe, he suggested, they could pay by installments. The Carters did not say much, partly because they did not know the size of the bill he was visualizing. Finally he sent them to take care of some business in a nearby office.

When they returned to talk to the receptionist, Dr. Matlock was nowhere in sight. The receptionist said, "There's no charge for today's visit. You're being referred to Dr. Bradford for a biopsy, and he *will* charge you!" At home, the Carters sent Dr. Matlock a card thanking him and admitting, "You judged us right; we do pinch. But the Lord helps us pay our bills, so we weren't too worried."

Two weeks later the Carters found themselves in Dr. Bradford's office, and again they stated that they did not have insurance. Dr. Bradford examined Mrs. Carter, decided not to do a biopsy, and said matter-of-factly, "I won't charge you for today's visit." They sent him a thank-you card too, quoting the verse, "He that watereth shall be watered also himself."

Score: three doctors—thirty dollars.

The surgery and hospital bills did turn out to be expensive in the end, and the church helped the Carter family. But by tokens, such as the things that happened beforehand, the Lord helped to increase their faith.

rather than running to him every time we get into a bind.

By the way, if the money to pay for our troubles comes out of our brethren's pockets, we should sense an obligation to keep the risks down. Buying an expensive car looks different once we realize that if we smash it, church friends will help to pay for it. Maybe we want to buy a cheaper one instead.

Medical Discounts

Times have changed. Years ago when you went to the hospital, you got a bill and you paid it. These days, hospitals function more like businesses. It is right to ask about prices and get information about discounts.

One reason hospital costs are high is because the hospital administrators know that in most cases they will end up giving discounts. Insurance companies give hospitals no choice; they simply state how much they will pay for a particular surgery or procedure. Individuals normally do not have that much arm-twisting power, nor would we as Christians use it if we had it. Still, while remaining friendly and respectful, we can do a few things to keep costs down.

For non-emergencies, negotiate ahead of time. Hospitals regard self-pay patients as high risks, but they give hefty discounts to people who pay up front. Agree with the hospital that what you are paying is the sum total and that no more will need to be paid. This helps prevent bills from coming to your desk like a never-ending swarm of bees. Even for emergencies, see what can be worked out on the day the patient enters the hospital.

One region (unfortunately, a small one) gives discounts to certain church members who have a religious exemption from social security. The logic is simple: people minded to waive their social security benefits are the type who band together to make sure each other's medical bills get paid on time and in full, and they will not bring lawsuits. Maybe churches in other regions can negotiate something similar.

Hospitals sometimes offer a charity plan for poor patients, which covers as much as 100 percent of the bill. This is funded by the hospital, the community, and the government. Should we take part in it? Hardly, if we belong to a church whose avowed purpose is to help each other with expenses. We accept business discounts, yes, but we take care of the charitable part ourselves. Hospitals themselves agree that this plan is not for us. Besides, why should the hospitals help our poor members while we help the rich ones?

In some regions, local people have formed a power bloc dedicated to bringing hospital costs down. But their tactics make Golden Rule Christians uncomfortable. Statements in their ads like "We put the heat on them!" sound foreign to the language in the Sermon on the Mount.

Taxes

Taxes are a way of paying back the country we live in for the privileges and protections we enjoy in it. For most readers, those privileges are considerable.

An accountant told of calculating the income tax for a married couple who had recently moved into the United States. The figure was quite high, and the accountant was concerned about how they might react. When he finally told them the figure, the husband turned to the wife and said, "It's a small price to live in this country."

Everyone knows, of course, that governments do not always do a good job of giving privileges and protections to their citizens. But the fact remains that we are better off with government than without it. "He is the minister of God to thee for good" (Romans 13:4). Therefore, "Render to Caesar the things that are Caesar's" (Mark 12:17).

Are there exceptions to this rule? Some people think so. Individuals have been known to calculate the military portion of certain taxes and withhold an equal portion. But Jesus lived under a militaristic government and could have mentioned that idea if He had thought it a good one. All He said was, "Render to Caesar . . ." Finally, we are not responsible for what the government does with our tax money, because once we have paid the tax, the money is no longer ours.

Some people seem to take exception to the whole concept of income taxes. They take the attitude, "The taxes aren't fair, and they are too high anyway, and I can use that money a whole lot better than the government can." Many people actually cheat to avoid paying the tax.

Yet in studying income taxation, one is impressed at how fair-minded the people in government actually are. They try to levy taxes so that no undue burden falls heavily on anyone. If they find that they have overlooked some people, they try again.

> *"The almost epidemic proportions that tax evasion has reached through non-reporting of all sources of income is one of our country's major economic woes."*[23]

For example, the United States has a graduated income tax, which means the more income you have, the higher the percentage you have to pay on your income. This is considered to be fair because the higher your income, the more you have left to live on even after you have paid a higher tax.

Now suppose you earn twice as much next year as you did this year. According to the way income tax is set up, you would pay a higher percentage on your income. Suppose, however, that the reason your income is higher is because of inflation, and prices have also doubled. You are no better off financially, yet you must give the government a larger piece of your pie than before.

To avoid this, the United States government keeps adjusting its tax requirements so that even after inflation, people pay the same amount on their real income as they had paid the year before. This is very considerate of the tax planners.

The government has also arranged that taxpayers already heavily burdened may pay little or no income tax. People with many children or other dependents, or people who have to pay a considerable amount in medical bills, or those who contribute much to a church or charity, are granted some tax relief. These are just a few examples.

Since the government provides legal ways to make your taxes fair, it is perfectly right to find out what those ways are and to take advantage of them. Even the Supreme Court says so. "The legal right of a taxpayer to decrease the amount of what otherwise would be his taxes, or to altogether avoid them, by means which the law permits, cannot be doubted."[24]

What are some appropriate ways to avoid paying too much income tax?

Have your taxes done by an accountant until you are confident of your own skills. One accountant made the remark that he likes to save people as much in taxes as he charges them for his services. It is not clear that this particular accountant was always able to do that honestly, but in many cases, no doubt he could. An accountant can tell you things you did not even know that you did not know.

Learn to fill out your own forms. The biggest work involved in tax preparation is keeping records and collecting information. You have already done that. Why not take the final step too?

Pull out last year's income tax form. Generally you can figure out why your accountant entered the figures he did. Now simply do the same on this year's form, following the same reasoning. Most of this year's figures will be fairly close to last year's. If an entry last year was $6,000 and this year it comes to $18, you probably erred somewhere. Go back over your calculations.

You might want to do everything in pencil and have your accountant check over it. He will probably compliment you on your efforts, spot-check your work, give you a few tips, and send you along with his blessing.

Any tax year you face extra complications (for example, you move), you can always check with the accountant again. One thing about filling out the tax forms yourself is that you become a little more intelligent about what is going on, and a little more confident when you are sitting across the desk from the accountant.

Learn to make judgment calls, having gotten good advice first, of course. This is a strange concept to many people. Someone sent the same income tax information to several different accountants to see if they would come up with the same figure on how much tax he owed. No doubt to his delight, he got as many different answers as there were accountants. What he failed to understand was that figuring out tax involves weighing various factors and making judgments on them. It is not a simple arithmetic problem.

For instance, suppose you take a trip to visit relatives and also take part in a week of church activities. For taking part, you receive several hundred dollars. You report that money as income. May you deduct the cost of transportation from that figure?

The law says you must determine the primary purpose of your trip. Was it to visit relatives, or was it to take part in church activities? If it was to visit relatives and the church activities were incidental, you should bear the cost of transportation yourself. If it was to take part in church activities and the visiting was incidental, you undertook the trip for the sake of the activities and may rightfully deduct expenses from the income.

It is easy to see that such a question does not have a simple answer. You may not really know which was more important. You would have visited the relatives even without the activities, and you would have taken part in the activities even without visiting relatives. (After all, you have served the church at other places where there were no relatives.) You can make a case for either side.

When deciding such questions, many people automatically give themselves the benefit of the doubt. But other people are not comfortable with judgment calls and automatically decide in favor of the government. They have to be reminded that it is all right to work within gray areas and make reasonable allowances for themselves.

Of course, you must be at peace with yourself and God about what you do. But that peace need not be based on the assurance that if you are ever audited, the auditor will not find a single thing he disagrees with. He just might, no matter how careful you are. And if he does, he will not cast you into prison. He will point out your error and have

> *"Sometimes an accountant must be as much a theologian as a mathematician."*

you pay your back taxes. It is only flagrant tax evasion that gets people into big trouble. We assume you are not guilty of that.

Neither do you want to be presumptuous. Once a young man bought a piece of ground from his grandfather. The realtor proposed that they make it a two-step process to avoid transfer taxes. Since the property would not be taxed if passed from father to son, the grandfather could sell it to his son, and the son to *his* son.

The proposal would have been legal. But would it have been right? Not everyone was sure. In the end, they did it the safe way. The grandfather sold the property directly to the grandson, and they paid the taxes.

The most important thing is not to do something that worries you afterward just enough that (years later) you finally give up trying to forget it and decide to make "restitution," simply to put it behind you.

"Since 1811, when James Madison was president, the U.S. Treasury has had a conscience fund. In that year some anonymous sender who wanted to clear his conscience of some public thievery sent in $5. Since that time [millions of dollars have] been sent in, ranging all the way from a dime which the finder didn't know what else to do with to the $50,000 which someone from Mississippi sent without explanation. The senders are often people who have cheated on their income tax, military personnel or government workers who pilfered government supplies, or persons who took items large or small from public places, such as railways or bus stations. One writer confided, 'About 58 years ago I took from a railroad station an item worth about $25, and this has been on my conscience since. So I am enclosing $50 to clear my conscience.'"[25]

Should you use the conscience fund for a simple mistake? Probably not. You can file an amended return if the mistake is large. For a minor error, you could simply add an appropriate amount to your tax figure next year.

Find tax-sheltered investments. Investments such as IRAs are evaluated elsewhere in this book (see pages 148–150). Here we will simply observe one of the smaller blessings of having children—they save you money in April! In fact, as dependents, they might completely wipe out your income tax.

Are there legal ways to reduce income taxes that we should *not* take? Many Christians feel uneasy about accepting money outright from the government. We are more comfortable with deductions than with subsidies, such as the Canada Child Tax Benefit. Reducing our taxes or getting a refund is one thing; getting money we never paid in is another.

One writer beating the subsidy drum says, "A Credit Beats a Deduction. . . . Unlike other credits, the earned income credit can be taken as a refund, even if you pay no taxes. Full instructions are with the Form 1040. In a simple case of a married couple with two children and an income of $11,000, no tax is payable, but the earned income credit comes back as a $3,110 refund check.

"Similarly, in Canada, provincial tax credits, federal Child Tax Benefits and sales tax credits can come back as refunds even if you pay no income tax."[26]

That is the kind of thing many conservative Christians like to stay away from.*

Consider reducing your income. The bigger the income, the bigger the tax bite, as noted a few pages back. This is an easy thing to ignore because the money is removed from your wages (if you are employed) before you ever see it. The fact is, it is money out of your pocket, and a sizable amount at that. When you get a raise, you have reason to ask who really got the raise—you or the government.

You smile at this? Then try using gross figures for budgeting, rather than using take-home pay figures. You will probably agree

---

* **Note:** There is a very important fact about the earned income credit that many people do not realize. This credit is a partial refund of FICA (social security) taxes to low-income people. So if you have a Form 4029 exempting you from social security tax, **you are not entitled to take the earned income credit**—not as a credit against your taxes, and especially not as a refund if the credit exceeds your tax liability.

that for many of us, our biggest single expense is taxes.

Therefore, it is right to consider how to reduce our income. That sounds strange until we consider that there are ways to provide for ourselves without having much money pass through our hands, if we can support ourselves in other ways. For just one option, consider having a vegetable garden. So far the government has not been taxing us on the peas we raise ourselves. No peas taste better than our own anyway.

See also "The tax benefits of living savingly," pages 79 and 80.

Consider incorporating if you have a business, even a small business. Taxes may be lower for a corporation. An employee pays taxes on his income before he spends anything. A corporation pays taxes on its income *after* it spends.[27]

Brave the arithmetic. Throughout the year, keep track of any expenses that you might be able to deduct from your taxes (such as vehicle expenses and medical bills). Once you are filling out the forms, do not get tired of calculating too soon. If backing up and recalculating for an hour saves you just twenty dollars, that is twenty dollars an hour. At the time of this writing, that is not a bad wage.

Making a Will

"We didn't need a will until now," said an elderly man to the lawyer preparing his will. Indeed, he did not need it even then, for no one needs a will until he is dead. But common sense should tell us that the time to make a will is before death rather than afterward. The patriarch Isaac had the right idea when he said, "I know not the day of my death" (Genesis 27:2). Neither do we, young or old.

Who should make a will? Anyone who owns things he cares about. If he owns nothing but has a spouse or children, he will need a will to make his wishes for them legally binding. If he does not have a proper will, the state will take over and make decisions, and the state's decisions may or may not be what the deceased person would have desired.

Who should draw up the will? You can, if the will is very simple and if you know how to make your wishes known in plain, simple language. However, it is quite likely that anything homemade will not hold good. Go to a local attorney, who knows his way through the legal jungle in your state, and do it his way.

Since you will not be able to put your will into effect once you are dead, you will need to ask someone to serve as executor. That person could be your husband or wife; but since you and your spouse could die in a common accident, it is wise to ask another person or persons as well. Preferably, an executor should be younger than you, since it is assumed that he will outlive you. If your will is simple, a relative or close friend might serve well. But if you have a business or large sum of money that must be professionally cared for, you will want to appoint someone qualified for that responsibility.

> "'You can't take it with you,' but that is no reason for leaving it in a mess."[28]

You will also want to ask someone to serve as guardian for your children. The executor cannot do this unless you specifically appoint him for this task. A guardian will not necessarily need to take your children under his own roof, but he or she will make sure your wishes for them are carried out. Since the guardian will take some responsibility for your children's spiritual nurture, choose carefully. (This is no doubt the most important reason to make a will; a state-appointed administrator might not make choices for your children that fall in line with your Christian principles.) As with the executor, take time to sit down and discuss these matters with the guardian.

Should you simply hand down to your children all the money you have? If you have a significant amount of money and they are under age, you will want to set up trust funds for the children so that the money stays in the control of the persons who care for them. Then too, you may wish to give some money to nonfamily recipients, such as the church.

Possessions other than money can cause awkwardness in the family. Which brother or sister gets what? If the possession is significant, such as the car or an old chest that has become an antique over the years, you might want to specify in your will who gets it. Smaller items, such as certain tools or the dieffenbachia plant, you might want to list on a separate, unofficial paper or leave to the discretion of the family.

Why wait to unload until you die? As you get older, you will want to start parting with your possessions, especially as you move into smaller quarters. You will have the satisfaction of seeing other people receive them. Besides, giving away any assets you can spare while you live will reduce taxes. Once you die, taxes on what you give to others will probably go up.

If you have funeral requests, your will may or may not be the place for them. Will relatives think to look in your will to find them? In any case, have a clear understanding with them. One man left directions for his funeral in his safe, and his widow could not get the safe open in time for the funeral.

Remember to review your will every year or two to make sure it still says what you want it to say.

The High Cost of Dying

Before considering the high cost of dying, maybe we should talk about the high cost of the dying process. Most of us can name elderly people whose medical and nursing care used up much or all of their savings and perhaps other people's too before they passed away. Uncle Fred was one such man. He and his family decided he would probably benefit from having heart bypass surgery. The surgery was successful, but he regretted the decision afterward because other health problems kept him in his sickbed, "too well to die and too sick to live." After his death, one of his sons remarked, "There were so many complications."

But electing *not* to have further surgery has its own hazards and complications. You cannot just go home, shake hands around the family circle, and die with a sigh. Yes, you can go home, but you do not know how long you might be a burden on your family.

In light of all this, we should be careful about making dry remarks criticizing elderly people who spend thousands of dollars on medical bills "in order to stay out of heaven." God does indeed want people to take care of themselves, so they should be willing to pay some medical bills. It is appropriate for them to spend some money to make their last days reasonably comfortable and even useful. It is not as simple an issue as dying or not dying.

Respect for human life also enters into consideration. Human life is sacred, and one should not carelessly endanger it or cast it away.

But even this issue has another side. Since human life is sacred, one should not stubbornly cling to it when God is asking to have it back. No one owns his own life; he merely borrows it—to keep carefully, but finally to give back to God.

A hundred years ago, doctors did all they could—which was never more than enough—to preserve life. These days doctors have the resources to extend life much longer than is warranted. Recognizing this, the United States Supreme Court ruled in 1990 that someone who has clearly stated that he does not want his life prolonged by artificial means should have his wishes respected.[29]

For this purpose, a person may draw up a living will, which states what kind of medical care he wants or does not want, in case he is too near death to communicate. For instance, he might state that he does not want to be placed on a respirator, or he does not want to be tube-fed, or he does not want his heart to be restarted artificially. Otherwise, the doctor might assume that he wants to be kept alive as long as possible.[30]

A similar arrangement is called a durable power of attorney. It puts the decisions about a person's care in the hands of a trusted person or persons.[31]

A local hospital can give you a form to fill out in making a living will. But remember that one can be overenthusiastic even in this. Feeding tubes and respirators are not just for prolonging people's lives needlessly. In many cases they give a patient time to recover.[32]

Sooner or later, however, all human life comes to its end. The funeral notice says the person has "entered into rest." Now what?

Without controversy, funerals are expensive. One book on finances talks about ten thousand dollars for a funeral. Maybe Joseph and Nicodemus spent the equivalent of that when they buried Jesus in fine linen and a hundred pounds of spices (Mark

15:46; John 19:39). But most of us will acknowledge a difference between burying the body of Jesus and burying well, supply your own name here. We can think of many better things that our family can do with ten thousand dollars (if they have that much) than saying good-bye to us after we are gone.

Of course, a human body deserves respect. And a funeral is not just for the one who has departed but also for the people who are left behind. There will be justifiable expenses. But just as certainly, we need to find a sensible approach to this. One church's "Rules and Discipline" puts it succinctly: "Gospel simplicity and economy should characterize our funerals."

Regrettably, the prevailing system works against us. The funeral home industry might seem like a racket,* but it seems to be one that society wants. Funeral homes are fine-to-luxurious because most customers want it that way. Hearses are modified luxury cars because people want it that way. How many people would patronize a funeral director whose hearse was a modified Volkswagen?

Maybe we should simply turn our backs on the system. The Amish people do. They make their own caskets—no, coffins—which are simple constructions that a skilled carpenter can build. They have their own horse-drawn hearses. They arrange things so that after the undertaker has prepared the body and brought it to the family home, his job is basically done.

What if we are not ready to go that far? Are there sensible things we can do to keep things simple and inexpensive? There are, and we should do some of them before a death actually occurs, especially when a person is likely to die in the near future. It is better to make some basic decisions at a neutral time than to decide everything at the time of a death.

We have a choice of caskets. Some are within range; some are out of this world. To make things complicated, some of the caskets that look simple, tasteful, and dignified are more expensive, and some that look rather gaudy are cheaper. The buyer has to find

---

* We should be cautious with such statements. Like other businesses, funeral homes have overhead costs that the casual observer does not think about.

an unhappy medium, which is one reason we should be slow to judge others for their choices.

Some of our own people can and do make caskets. The style is right, and the price is not far wrong. A casket, by its nature, is more expensive than a coffin, but at least the money for it goes into the pocket of a brother in the church.

An alternative to a casket might be a cremation box, even if there is no cremation. The box is simple in style and made of inexpensive wood.

We can do for ourselves what the funeral director would otherwise do—things like keeping and transporting the body, having the viewing somewhere other than in the funeral home, and directing the funeral and burial. As a matter of courtesy, there needs to be an understanding with the funeral director on these matters. Also, we should have a clear understanding about costs because some funeral directors charge the same flat fee whether or not we use all their services. The same might even apply to caskets.

There may be times to do it the funeral director's way even if that would not have been our first choice. When one group proposed to take the casket themselves from the funeral to the cemetery, a distance of some miles, the funeral director wondered why they would want the casket bouncing on the back of a pickup when hearse service would not cost much extra. They finally chose the hearse.

What about the matter of cremation? It is cheaper, yet many conservative Christians do not feel comfortable with the idea.[33] Achan the thief was burned as part of his punishment (Joshua 7:25). But Abraham, Isaac, and Jacob were each buried with honors. Of David, the apostle Peter said, "His sepulchre is with us unto this day" (Acts 2:29). Somehow, "His ashes are with us unto this day" would have a different ring.

All this is not to judge those who prefer to cremate and who believe it is just as respectful as burial. Those of us who live in the country and are used to spacious cemeteries should remember that dwellers in crowded cities might have practical reasons to cremate. But the most applicable Scripture for many of us would be, "All things are lawful for me, but all things edify not" (1 Corinthians 10:23).

There are other expenses, such as the cost of the burial plot and the gravestone, plus the digging of the grave. Often this comes on top of hospital expenses, the cost of phone calls and transportation, and the temporary or permanent loss of income. The church should be conscious of these stresses on the bereaved, especially for those with a limited income. We should remember that we are here "in Christ's stead" and should seek to exercise the mind of Christ.

4. Investing

A certain miser kept his money hidden in a hole. Periodically he would take it out and gloat over it, then put it back in the hole. One evening he went to find his money and discovered that someone had stolen it. He set up such a wail that the neighbors came running. On learning what his trouble was, one of the neighbors asked, "What did you intend to do with the money?"

"Nothing," sniffed the miser. "I just wanted to look at it."

"Well, in the future," the neighbor advised, "why don't you just look at the hole? It will do you just as much good."

Jesus told a similar story. In this case, a man received a talent of money to be invested, but he hid it in a hole. When accounting day came, the man told his master that he had played it safe. His angry master replied, "Thou oughtest therefore to have put my money to the exchangers, and then at my coming I should have received mine own with usury" (Matthew 25:27). In other words, "If you wanted to play it safe from my disapproval, you should at least have put it where it would have earned a little interest." In the end, the man lost talent, interest, and all.

God has given us intangible assets, such as life, love, time, and aptitudes, and we ought to be investing them. But in this chapter we want to think especially about investing tangible things—our money and possessions. As we proceed, however, it should become obvious that the tangible and the intangible have a good bit to do with each other.

"Think Big"

"Where no oxen are, the crib (stall) is clean: but much increase is by the strength of the ox" (Proverbs 14:4). Does the first part of the verse mean that if you do not have an ox, you do not have to keep corn in the crib to feed him? Or does it mean that without an ox you do not even have corn to put in the crib?

In any case, the last part of the verse is clear. "Much increase is by the strength of the ox." An ox is worth the investment. He is worth what it costs to buy him, and he is worth what it costs to feed him. He brings in more than he takes out. He earns his keep.

George once went to his neighbors' garage sale and saw that they were offering a garden tiller. The cost was about seventy-five dollars. Being a penny pincher, George passed up the tiller and kept the money in his pocket.

There was only one problem—the tilling had to be done in some other way. The next spring George hired a man to work up his garden for him. Guess what he paid—about seventy dollars! The money he had saved was practically all gone, and he had no tiller to show for it.

George has plenty of company. A certain man had a machine that needed to be fixed and was wasting oil. But the man kept saying that fixing it was too expensive. So he kept buying oil, and in so doing he dumped more money into his problem than he ever would have spent on getting the thing fixed.

Like many others, the man was being penny wise and dollar foolish. Instead of asking himself, "Can I afford to repair this?" he should have been asking, "Can I afford not to?"

Writers invest in computers. It does not help them to write much faster, but they can edit faster, and once that is done they do not have to retype it. Much increase is by the strength of the computer.

I am not saying this to encourage people to buy computers. Some people have convictions against owning them, just as you and I have convictions against owning certain things. But it is another matter to drag your feet simply because you do not feel like spending money for something that would actually be a great help.

There is another side to this, of course. Some people buy "oxen" to do a rabbit's job. They buy computers to keep track of their checkbooks when hand-held calculators would do about as well and give them more room on their desktops. They buy riding mowers to cut their city lawns, and snowblowers to clear their driveways two or three times a winter, even if they do not have a heart condition. Truly, "you can tell the men from the boys by the price of their toys."

But to come back to the point. We need to "think big" when it is time to think big. Remember what Elisha told the widow in financial trouble. "Go, borrow thee vessels abroad of all thy neighbours, even empty vessels; *borrow not a few*" (2 Kings 4:3).

Consider also the Shunammite woman who gave Elisha a standing invitation to drop in whenever he passed by. After he had done that a number of times, she proposed to her husband that they build another room onto the house so that they could accommodate Elisha better. She could think big.

The point is that the maxim, "If you watch your pennies, the dollars will take care of themselves" can backfire. If you do not even invest in a putty knife, how will you patch your roof? If you try to save money by not buying good tires when you need them, how far will your savings go in paying for a major accident?

There is a time to pinch pennies. But there is also a time to make things happen with dollars by investing them. "Nothing ventured, nothing gained" applies both to spiritual things and to natural things. "He which soweth sparingly shall reap also sparingly; and he which soweth bountifully shall reap also bountifully" (2 Corinthians 9:6).

Investing Defined

In the old countrified days, you knew where to invest your money. It was in your farm and all that went with it—equipment, seed, cows, chickens, hogs, fruit trees. Your farm in turn produced corn, milk, eggs, bacon, apples, cherries, and more.

Along with your money, you invested time and labor. You could not merely buy a cow. You had to provide her with hay and other feed, treat her for mastitis, fix her hoof, dodge her switching tail, milk her, strain the milk, cool the milk, and skim the milk before you finally had cream to pour over your apple pie. And the apples in the pie? Same story. The apple trees had to be planted, defended from mice and deer, sprayed for pests, and finally picked before your wife made the pie.

Those were the days when you worked for your farm and your farm worked for you. Labor and investment had married each

Not everything you spend money on is an investment. Buying a bed for yourself is not an investment, because you do not expect any monetary return from the bed. If you were running a bed-and-breakfast and bought a bed that people would pay to sleep in, that would be an investment.

Someone is sure to argue that buying a bed for yourself is an investment in a sense because it pays for itself by refreshing you and preparing you for another day's work. Very well, buying a bed is an investment *in a sense*, just like buying a good pair of shoes or even buying a dozen eggs, but it is not the kind of investment we are talking about here.

other, and you had a pretty good concept of them both because both were imposed on you.

These days, labor and investment often still go hand in hand, though not necessarily on a farm. Take for example the owner-operator of a backhoe. He has put considerable money into that piece of machinery. Now he sits in the machine hour after hour and works along with his investment. His money is working for him, but he is also working.

In many cases, it is not obvious that labor and investment work hand in hand, but they do. You might labor on someone else's investment, and someone else might labor on yours. For example, you might get your paycheck from working in Oberholtzer's greenhouse, and then turn around and invest part of that check in your friend Paul's new dairy barn. Your labor and your investment seem to be divorced from each other. Yet after a moment's thought, you can see that you are laboring on someone else's investment and investing in someone else's labor. The two are still tied together.

Sometimes the labor is so far removed from the investment that you can hardly track it down. If you put money in the bank, the bank might lend it to businesses unknown to you that provide jobs for workers unknown to you. Still, the connection is there.

Is there such a thing as labor that involves no investment? Hardly. Practically any worker needs tools or a desk or at least some square footage on which to work—either his own or someone else's. Someone had to invest in it.

Is there such a thing as investment that involves no labor? That is an interesting question because we sometimes hear the

114

advice, "Don't work for money; let money work for you."

> "If everyone jumps onto the bandwagon, who will pull the wagon?"

It would be more accurate to say, "Work for money *and* let money work for you." If no one worked for money, then money would stop working. We are in no danger of that happening, but we have all seen a modified form of it. The less people work for a dollar, the less the dollar works for them, and the more inflation there is. Other factors cause inflation too, but this is one of them. We are back to the fact that investment involves labor.

Still, some people keep being fascinated by the idea of pulling money out of thin air without working for it. There is in fact a way to do this. But now we are not talking anymore about *investing*. We are talking about *speculating*.

Speculating Defined

Remember, investment involves patience and hard work. By some people's standards, the profits involved in investing are low. But then the risks are low too.

> "There are two times not to speculate—when you can't afford it, and when you can."[1]

Speculating is quite different. It is a particular temptation to rich people. Working people know they do not have much margin for error, so they do not want to risk whatever money they have worked so hard to earn. But the rich know that even if they play with money, losing money will not wipe them out. Besides, some of them have not worked hard for their money and do not know its value in terms of labor.

Some speculators take over corporations by buying more than half of the stock in them. Since stockholders control the corporation, as soon as the speculators hold 51 percent of the stock, they can call the shots. If they want to merge two corporations that they own, and then lay off a third of the employees, they can do it. Speculators can be cold-blooded.

Some speculators play the stock market. They watch market trends closely and know when to buy and when to sell. By clever trading, they can sometimes win huge profits in minutes.

> *"The meek shall inherit the earth." The assertive might grab some of it, but they never keep it for long.*

And some people are wannabe speculators, who really know little about the game but want to try their own hand at buying and selling stocks. Perhaps the most tragic example of this came in October 1929. People were borrowing money to invest in stocks; and when the stock market crashed, they lost everything—in fact, many lost more than they owned.

Does avoiding speculation mean that we try to evade all risk? No—and no one knows that better than a farmer. Frost, drought, pestilence, and the uncertainties of market prices certainly constitute risks. Farming has its windfalls too, when things go especially well. For these reasons, some people think of farming as a gamble.

But it is not a gamble, really. While farming is a lesson in life's uncertainties, it is also a lesson in the certainties of life—the change of the seasons, the principle that life comes from life, and above all, the certainty that God is watching and smiles upon a faithful laborer. A tradesman or day laborer understands many of these things too. Somehow, a speculator misses all these lessons.

Gambling

The little store at the gas station explodes with cheers. "Hey, Dad, you finally did it! Three hundred dollars!" A gentleman stands there grinning, watching the cashier hand over the money. In the window a sign tells the story: "Play here! We pay here!"

Off to one side a customer watches with interest. He figures it would be easier to persuade lightning to strike him than to win the lottery; but at the moment, the euphoria affects him too. Three hundred dollars—what couldn't he buy with that! Gas for his tank, for one thing.

"Now, what else can we do for you today?"

The lottery winner, still glowing, says, "Well, this'll pay for my gas today. Also I'd like to buy some more lottery tickets. This is my lucky day, so maybe I'm on a real winning streak." Before he moves off the spot, he has handed eighty dollars back over the counter.

The quiet customer finally gets his turn at the counter, thinking. He buys no tickets.

I assume you do not gamble, but why not?

The most obvious reason is that you stand to lose more than you gain. The gentleman who won the lottery had no doubt already spent more than he ever won. Very few people get more out of gambling than they put in.

A second reason? Gambling warps the character. Many people overlook this. They assume that if assured they would win the lottery, it would be a great thing to play. Or they say, "I put in only a dollar or two a week. For me, it's cheap fun." (Jesus would have said, "Verily I say unto you, you have your reward—cheap fun!") The fact is that gambling fosters the something-for-nothing mentality. Gambling is speculation at its worst.

A third reason? The Bible gives it: "Wealth gotten by vanity shall be diminished" (Proverbs 13:11). A few lottery winners use their newfound wealth to do a fair amount of good. But studies indicate that most end up no better off than they were, or worse. People who are suddenly wealthy often do not know how to handle that wealth—especially if, like the gentleman in the story above, they are the type who play the lottery.

A fourth reason for not gambling? The embarrassment of winning! The bigger the win, the bigger the embarrassment. Would you like to see your name in the paper under the headline, "Local Citizen Wins a Million"? No, especially if you make an obvious profession of religion. You know how a headline like "Amish Man Wins a Million" would strike the public. The same principle applies to you, Amish or otherwise.

A fifth reason: gambling violates the Golden Rule. "Gambling is always contrary to love and is motivated by greed because a man seeks, to the harm of another, what does not belong to him."[2] If that is not clear to you, consider where the money comes from that a gambler garners at a casino. Is it not from the pockets of other gamblers who lost their money? He did not do them a single service for their money that now resides in his pocket.

Can gambling create wealth? No, it just rearranges wealth. Governments hungry for cash sponsor lotteries, and with the revenue from it they do some good for the people. But who provided the money? It came from the customers of local stores who no longer buy as much because they cannot afford it. They put that money into gambling.

Now, a word to the non-gamblers. Are there ways to gamble other than by means of lotteries and casinos? One way is to simply bump along, hoping that something good will turn up. As a rule, it will not. What about the saying, "All things come round to him who will but wait"? That is not always true. Even if you "get lucky" once in a while, you will not know what to do with your good fortune. Someone who works hard and never looks for luck is more likely to have great things happen and to benefit from them. Life is governed by predictable laws; and if you work by them, you will succeed.

In an old book called *Getting One's Bearings,* the author says, "To make the most of Now is to be most ready for Tomorrow."[3] And again: " 'He is always lucky,' we say. True, but he is always faithful. 'Fortune is on his side.' True, but he has chosen to be on the side of fortune. He chose the course upon which fortune would naturally smile. . . . There must be hazard if there is to be gain; but it is the hazard of foresight and discretion, not the hazard of dice."[4]

Finally, "He that maketh haste to be rich shall not be innocent" (Proverbs 28:20). Also, "He that hasteth to be rich hath an evil eye, and considereth not that poverty shall come upon him" (Proverbs 28:22).

Ironically, people can work harder at not working than they would work if they actually worked. The following story may be fictitious, but it makes a good point.

A young fellow was not interested in working. He preferred to make his living by betting on horseraces. After making a fair amount of money at the races, he took sick. The doctor checked him out and said it looked like a case of overwork. Of course, the young fellow had not worked at all, but the diagnosis made him think. He tallied up his hours at the races and compared them with the amount of money he had made. Surprise! He found that he would be just as well off if he worked at doing something useful as if he continued his chosen "trade."

Futures Trading

Suppose a farmer expects to harvest a good crop of wheat in another month. However, he fears that the price of wheat will drop by that time because all the other farmers will be harvesting good crops of wheat too. So he finds someone who does not mind promising to buy his crop of wheat at a stated price a month from now. Then the farmer can relax. By selling on futures, he will not get as high a price as he might get if he is wrong about a decline in the price of wheat. But neither will he be left with a bumper crop that he is obliged to sell at a pittance. Now he can plan financially because his future is more secure. Locking in a price for a crop ahead of time is called *hedging*.

Now suppose that a month later this farmer is delighted with the price he gets for his wheat because he would otherwise have gotten much less. His next reaction is to think, "Smart buying and selling is as profitable as farming, and it's much less work! I should have agreed to sell neighbor Jones's crop of wheat, too, at a guaranteed price. I could be buying it from him now and selling it at a profit."

At this point the farmer should realize that he is no longer looking at hedging but at speculating. He is no longer interested in getting a good price for the fruit of his labor. Rather, he is seeking to make a profit by playing a money game. If he persuades himself to pursue this, he might decide to quit farming, buy a computer, get a direct line to the Chicago Board of Trade, and do nothing but trade commodities. He could trade in foreign currencies on the same market because their prices also keep rising and falling, as well as in precious metals for the same reason. All he has to do is outguess the market.

If anyone points out to him that he is gambling, he can quickly point out that he is doing a service to the economy. If enough people do what he is doing, they help to stabilize commodity prices, keeping them from soaring unrealistically high or sinking disastrously low. But despite the supposed benefit, speculating is wrong. If enough people speculate, they can *de*-stabilize prices too.

Besides, the farmer who merely plays the market wants to

get money without creating wealth. He wants to take advantage of the mistakes of others, which is not a Christian thing to do. Hedging—protecting the price of something one has worked hard to produce—is one thing. Speculating—playing with the price of commodities other people have worked hard to produce—is quite another.

Finally, speculating in the futures market can be extremely dangerous. In 1995 a British bank collapsed (it was one of the oldest in the world) when one of its traders in Singapore lost over a billion dollars by trading in the futures market.[5]

Stocks and Bonds

Stocks. Buying stocks means investing in a company. Suppose four brothers want to go into a business together. To get the business up and running, each brother invests in the business the amount of money he can afford. When the business starts bringing in profits, each brother receives a percent of the profits proportional to his share. In other words, if a brother owns a third of the business, he gets a third of the profits. If he owns a twentieth, he gets a twentieth.

Moreover, if the business prospers and grows, each brother's share expands along with the business. If a brother has invested ten thousand dollars in the business, what happens if the total amount of the company's money doubles over the years? His share doubles too. Now he has twenty thousand dollars.

Suppose one of the brothers becomes very enthusiastic about the business and wishes he held a greater share in it. Fred might go to Sam and say, "Would you be interested in selling some of your share in the business?" Sam is slightly less optimistic about the future of the business, so he says, "I really don't want to sell because the future of the business looks good. But I need some cash just now; so if you buy a thousand dollars' worth of my share in the business for $1,200, I'll let you have it." Fred says, "It's a deal! I'll get my money out of it sooner or later, even if I pay the higher price."

This, in simplified form, is the way a large business works.

Only instead of four brothers, there are thousands of investors. By buying shares called stocks, they become part owners in the company. Periodically they receive money called dividends on their investments.

When times are good, many investors become excited. They want to buy more stocks, and they will pay a higher price than the stocks originally cost. Sometimes prices of stocks go unrealistically high—much higher than the actual shares of the business that they represent. When anything happens to make investors doubt that the company will continue doing well, the price of stocks in that company will fall. If something happens to cause a drastic, widespread loss of confidence in many companies, there is a corresponding drastic, widespread drop in the price of stocks. In other words, the stock market crashes.

> *One reason why the Great Depression followed the crash of 1929 was that most investors no longer wanted to invest. Companies were crippled for lack of capital.*

Is there anything wrong with investing in a company? Not with the basic idea. If you were one of the four brothers mentioned earlier, you would think it proper to invest in your own company. Investing in someone else's company is not much different. Investment—true investment—is good and healthy.

Now if investment is good, why do so many good people shy away from the stock markets? Their reputation is such that one widely read magazine made a statement something like this: "If you want to make money, hold your nose and go to Wall Street."

First, we should understand that there are two kinds of stock—common stock and preferred stock. Owners of preferred stock are safer because they get paid before owners of common stock. On the other hand, they get only a specified rate of interest. Common stock owners live in a more exciting world. They might get no returns at all, or they might get a hefty sum. When people speak of the stock market, they usually have common stock in mind.

One of the main objectionable things is that the stock market is full of money-hungry people, who are out to make large, fast profits. If they merely created their own disasters, they might be pardoned, but their maneuvering can send shock waves through the economy of the whole world.

For instance, some years ago the Canadian dollar lost a great deal of value. Why? Speculators thought that Canadian exporters were about to lose Pacific buyers of their raw materials because South Korea, Indonesia, Malaysia, and other countries were going through a major economic crisis. So the speculators quickly sold many Canadian dollars that they were holding. As it turned out, Canada's markets did not suffer as much as expected, but the speculation with Canadian dollars did erode the value of Canada's money. The speculators created the very scenario they had envisioned. This harmed people who needed a more predictable world in which to operate.[6]

The stock market illustrates all too vividly that "riches certainly make themselves wings; they fly away as an eagle toward heaven" (Proverbs 23:5). Companies do go bankrupt. Near the end of 2001, the largest bankruptcy in American history took place. Many employees had bought into the doomed Enron Corporation, but they lost their life savings.

Then what about buying preferred stock instead of common stock?

This is safer, but common stock and preferred stock have a similar problem. Buying stock in a company amounts basically to accepting partial ownership of that company. You may be entitled to help elect a board of directors, thus taking partial responsibility for company policy.[7] The Bible says, "Be ye not unequally yoked together with unbelievers. . . . Wherefore come out from among them, and be ye separate, saith the Lord, and touch not the unclean thing" (2 Corinthians 6:14, 17). Holding part ownership in a company would mean taking partial responsibility for its sub-Christian practices. Holding shares in a local business operated by Christians would be different.

Bonds. Stocks and bonds are different in nature. When you buy bonds, you simply lend to a business or government rather than becoming a part owner. Christians have fewer problems with bonds than with stocks. However, there are still some questions.

United States savings bonds are one example. During World War I, a number of Christians got into trouble for refusing to buy war bonds. They did not want their money to support that kind of enterprise. Are United States savings bonds different nowadays?

Here is an interesting observation: "Having first emerged into prominence during the Second World War, savings bonds have always been associated with patriotism, which has ensured a steady demand for them over the years."[8] Hmm.

Municipal bonds, then? You can invest in specific projects like the building of roads, bridges, and schools.[9] Some of those projects would seem to be worthwhile. And they are tax-exempt.

If not municipal bonds, perhaps corporate bonds? These are more risky than municipal bonds but have higher rates of return.[10]

We are back to the same old question, which is not, "Where can I find a good place to invest my money?" The question is rather, "Where is the *best* place?"

Mutual Funds

Is investing in mutual funds better than buying stocks? Well, even with mutual funds, you are probably buying stocks indirectly. But this time, instead of making your own decisions, you are turning your money over to a company that invests it for you. Their experts have done more homework than you have time to do and presumably can make wiser choices. Naturally, the company charges a fee for its services.

Investing in mutual funds is relatively safe because your money is dispersed in a variety of places. Your eggs go into many baskets. If part of a mutual fund is invested in a company that goes bankrupt, the fund still has money in many others.

Also, mutual funds are relatively lucrative because the experts are getting money from hundreds of people besides yourself and investing theirs along with yours. With all that money, they can make huge, profitable investments that you alone cannot afford.

The downside?

Mutual fund holders can lose too, and it is small comfort that they

> *Money market funds are mutual funds especially for short-term savers. Money market managers lend to short-term borrowers, such as the government, banks, and corporations.*

would all lose together. In 1995 one observer mused, "We are facing the greatest risk of a stock market crash since 1929. At the same time, millions of naïve, inexperienced investors are pouring their life savings into a staggering array of mutual funds."[11] He added, "The only ones who will win are those who were wise enough to move their funds out of the stock market and mutual funds before the economic collapse and financial panic sets in."[12] Dismiss his economic forecast if you like, but his portrayal of the character of the stock market is worth considering.

Also, the unequal-yoke specter is still there. A mutual fund holder is part owner of various companies, and he is partner with many other investors. Once again the question comes: "Is this the best way I can serve the Lord with my money?" Mutual fund experts do not worry about such matters. They just put your money wherever they think the most profits will be. Of course, you can partially answer your questions by choosing the type of mutual funds you want, but you cannot completely solve the problem.

Another teaching of Jesus needs to be considered in this matter of stocks, bonds, and mutual funds. "Lay not up for yourselves treasures upon earth, where moth and rust doth corrupt, and where thieves break through and steal: . . . for where your treasure is, there will be your heart be also" (Matthew 6:19, 21). Christians think more about investing in Kingdom work rather than in security. When security is our main concern, our treasure is on this earth, and our heart is there also. Christians want their treasures to be in heaven.

Before we look later in the chapter for a better place to invest, let us take a little detour.

The Eighth Wonder of the World

On a pocket calculator, enter **1.06 x 100** and press the = sign. You should get $106, the amount you would have in the bank after one year at 6 percent interest. Keep

"Get rich slowly."

on pressing the = sign and see how the number grows. How many years will it take to double the investment? You may be surprised to learn that it takes just twelve years. That is a fact—after you hit the = sign the twelfth time, the display shows **201.2196472.** That is $201.22 for leaving the money in the bank all that time and letting it accumulate compound interest.

We will go a little further. What will happen if you push the = sign twelve more times? You will get **404.8934641.** Once again the investment has doubled, which means that after twenty-four years in the bank, the balance is actually *four times* as high as the original amount.

After another twelve years the figure is **814.7252.** So if someone places $100 in savings at 6 percent compound interest at the age of twenty, and leaves it there until he is fifty-six, he will have *eight times* as much money. Do you see why compound interest has been called the eighth wonder of the world?

There is an interesting rule about interest called "the rule of 72." Divide 72 by the interest rate, and you have the approximate number of years in which the investment will double. Notice how that holds true in the example above. Divide 72 by 6 and you get 12, the number of years for an investment at compound interest to double.

There is another interesting fact about interest. Even more important than *how much* money you invest is *how long* you invest it.

According to "the rule of 72," $100 at 6 percent interest will become $200 in twelve years, as noted above. Let us quadruple the investment to $400 but keep the time the same. In twelve years the $400 investment will have grown to about $800.

Now then, quadruple the time but keep the amount at $100. In forty-eight years, $100 will amount to about $1,600. Multiplying the *time* by 4 makes the final amount twice as high as multiplying the *amount* by 4.

If the $24 that bought Manhattan Island in 1626 had been invested at 6 percent compound interest, it would have generated nearly 7 *billion* dollars by the year 2000.

By the way, you had better let the bank know from time to time that you are still interested in your account. If you let the money just sit there without making any deposits or withdrawals, your account will go dormant after several years. Then if the bank cannot get hold of you, it will finally turn the account over to the state. (In legal terms, the account will be *escheated* to the state.) The state will also try to track you down, but it will not pay you interest on the money it holds.

And Now for the Ninth Wonder

Using "the rule of 72" again, we will work with 18 percent interest. How soon will the investment double now? In just four years, because 72 divided by 18 is 4.

Do you say that is unrealistic because you never expect to get 18 percent interest? Maybe you will never get it, but you might be *paying* it. I just checked a recent credit card statement, and sure enough, the annual interest rate is 18.5 percent. Check your own statement if you have one, and see if it says something similar.

Why would anyone charge that much interest except out of pure greed? Well, credit card companies have expenses that we do not have to worry about. Credit card fraud is a big problem these days. People steal cards and go on shopping sprees, and the companies bear much of the loss for that. Then too, some people simply walk away from their credit card debts. Tracking them down and trying to make them pay (when they might have no money anyway) would cost more than bearing the loss. As the saying goes, "It isn't all gravy"—not even for credit card companies.

Although 18 percent interest is not pure gain for the credit card company, it is pure loss for the cardholder. An unpaid balance of one hundred dollars will become two hundred dollars in just four years—actually in a shorter time if there are fees and penalties.

Do you see why the government has trouble paying off its debts? And do you see why you should pay off your debts before the power of compounding interest works *against* you?

If only unpaid debt were the only drain that money can go down! Sorry, it is not. The Germans found that out after World War I. Inflation got so bad that employers routinely paid their employees partway through the day and gave them time off to buy things before prices went up again. The government finally took control of the situation, redeeming old money at the rate of one trillion old paper marks to one new mark.[13] Many people lost their life savings.

If the eighth wonder of the world is how fast money can accumulate, the ninth wonder must be how fast it can disappear. But that is not really a wonder. God told us about it a long time ago in the proverb quoted earlier about riches making themselves wings. Jesus said, "Lay not up for yourselves treasures upon earth, where moth and rust doth corrupt, and where thieves break through and steal" (Matthew 6:19).

The point of this is not that you should avoid investing. Rather, you should realize and accept the risks involved and invest in the safest things possible. Directly or indirectly, all your investments should contribute to the bank of heaven, "where neither moth nor rust doth corrupt, and where thieves do not break through nor steal" (Matthew 6:20).

Properties and Home Ownership

Many homeowners think of their homes as investments. Are they truly investments? Yes—and no.

In terms of personal satisfaction, owning might be better for you. You have a sense of "Here is where I belong, and no one will push me out." Furthermore, once you have paid for the house, you have a house. If you pay rent all those years, you end up with enough receipts to make a small roof, perhaps, but certainly not a house.

By owning your home, however, you do not gain as much monetarily as you might think. You have to pay upkeep expenses for which you will have nothing but receipts, the same as a renter. The same applies to taxes, and they can rise over time. A cartoon shows a house with a tree in front of it—a huge tree labeled "Property taxes." The owner is lamenting, "It was just a sapling when we moved here!"

If you invest your money in some venture other than a house, you will get greater returns, at least in terms of interest. Suppose you have fifty thousand dollars. If you invest it in a business, you might get ten percent a year, which is five thousand dollars. If you invest it in a house, you will lose all the interest you could have gotten over the years.

But suppose you don't have fifty thousand dollars, and you decide to borrow money to purchase the house. You will pay a goodly sum, say, a hundred thousand dollars (principal plus interest) for a fifty-thousand-dollar house, and you call it an investment! It seems that the only mathematical reason for buying a house is to avoid the alternative—paying rent all those years. Unless you are paying cash or unless you get all the money back out of your house that you actually put into it, a house is not really an investment.

Inflation sweetens the bitterness a little. If you buy a house during an inflationary period, inflation will keep nudging your income upward while your house payments remain the same. But in these uncertain days, one cannot even count on inflation. "There's no law that says real estate can't decrease in value."[14] Some people owe more on their homes than they could get back if they sold them.[15]

Even if you could justifiably call buying a house an investment, it will take up all your savings unless you are richer than most of us. Consequently, you cannot diversify. If your property loses value, the sum total of your investment will lose value too.

On a table, the pluses and minuses of buying and renting would look like this:

Buying	Renting
You have a house to show for it.	You still have your savings.
You earn no interest.	You can earn interest elsewhere.
You pay property taxes.	You have no property taxes.
You pay for repairs and utilities.	Maintenance is not a major worry.
You do not pay rent.	You pay rent.
You pay interest on the mortgage.	You pay no interest.
You benefit from fixing things up.	Fixing up benefits the landlord.
You may decorate as you please.	You may not!
Your dwelling is tax-sheltered.*	Your business investment may be taxed.
You will not be pushed out.	You never know.
You benefit from inflation.	You do not lose if inflation cools.
You are forced to save.	You gain nothing except a place to live.

---

* A person's primary dwelling is tax-sheltered in that it is exempt from capital gains tax (tax on its increasing value) up to a certain amount of gain, such as $250,000.

All things considered, the cost of owning comes close to the cost of renting. If buying had no advantages over renting, everyone would want to rent. If renting had no advantages over buying, everyone would buy. At least they would if they had any money. But even people with money sometimes rent.

The Church Brotherhood

By this time you can see that investing money in the business of a Christian brother has definite advantages.

Will the money be safe? As safe as the brotherhood is. They will back up your money with their own character. If interest rates soar, they might offer to pay you more. And if interest rates drop, you might offer to trim what you had originally agreed upon. If your debtor meets disaster through mismanagement, other brothers will take notice and try to prop him up or at least let him down easy, saving some of your money in the process. This warm family spirit is unheard of in the icy financial world. Normally if a company goes bankrupt, investors might as well accept the fact that they have lost their money.

> *"Lend, hoping for nothing again; and your reward shall be great" (Luke 6:35).* In context, this verse seems to be talking about helping out an ungodly neighbor. How much more should we help out someone who is of the household of faith?

Will the money be doing what you want it to be doing? With little doubt. If a brother borrows your money to expand his milking operation, your money will go for just that. This stands in contrast to putting your long-term money into some anonymous outfit whose products and policies you might not approve. By keeping the money within the brotherhood, you help your brother materially and spiritually. It is a way of laying up treasure in heaven.

If you have money to invest in the brotherhood but do not know where, just ask questions. Businessmen in the church have connections and can put you in touch with the needs.

The biggest drawback to investing in the brotherhood lies in the fact that it is not tax-sheltered or exempt from taxes. (Maybe some brotherhood enterprises are, or can be made so.) But we have already noted some advantages that outweigh this fact. Once again, the biggest plus is the eternal perspective. Even though compound interest has an astounding ability to accumulate, God knew all about compound interest long before humans discovered it. No one can outbid Him!

If God ever gets a twinkle in His eye, it must be when one of His children wonders if he should have invested his money in an earthly enterprise instead of giving it to the Lord. God's answer must be, "Don't you worry!"

Of course, there is no value in calculating everything we have ever given to the Lord, applying the principle of compound interest, and seeing how much we must have stashed away in heaven by this time. God does not operate that way. If He did, we would end up pitifully poor in heaven because most of the things found there are priceless.

An imaginary story tells of a man who begged God to let him take at least a bagful of his earthly treasures to heaven when he died. God finally promised to let him do so. Upon the man's arrival at the celestial gates, the angels saw his bag and said, "Sorry; nothing from earth may enter heaven."

"I've gotten special permission," replied the man, and he showed them that his bag was full of gold.

The angels took one look and said, "Pavement!"

But that story still comes a little short. According to Revelation 21:21, the gold of earth is nothing to compare with the gold of heaven. It is not fit even for pavement.

Already here on earth, God has given us many things that we could never buy with money. The company of good people, for one thing. A number of us have children, and we would not part with any one of them for a million dollars.

God does not owe us anything. He will not be bound by figures. If He stuck to arithmetic, we would come out the losers. He has already given us everything we have.

"We give Thee but Thine own,
Whate'er the gift may be;
All that we have is Thine alone,
A trust, O Lord, from Thee."

More About Lending
Within the Brotherhood

Lending within the church brotherhood is like lending within a family. Two blood brothers are often quite free with each other. James lends to John, and John lends to James. If John through some misfortune (not that he is careless) loses what he borrowed, James will love him anyway and perhaps bear the loss himself.

Still, it is wise to remember Shakespeare's oft-quoted advice.

Neither a borrower nor a lender be;
For loan oft loses both itself and friend,
And borrowing dulls the edge of husbandry.[16]

Misunderstandings and disagreements can arise even among honest people and take the shine off their friendship. Before you lend, think twice. Be slow to say, "Whatever you do with the money is fine with me because I'm sure it's in good hands." Ask friendly questions. Not only does it show interest in what the other person is doing, it also gives you important information.

Know where the would-be borrower is financially, how good a manager he is, and how faithful he is in keeping commitments. Get a second opinion from a levelheaded businessman if you need to. We can all profit from good advice.

Notice in the quotation above that "borrowing dulls the edge of husbandry." Possibly this means that if people know they can borrow, they tend to rely on that and fail to work hard for themselves. Or they do not take as good care of what they borrow as what they have worked for. Of course, this caution does not always hold true. But even fond fathers, bearing this in mind, can let their children be stuck a little to encourage them to provide for themselves. Sometimes this must happen in the brotherhood too.

A man who had known his share of hard times early in life finally began to prosper, only to learn that he had new questions to answer. Men would ask him for financial help, and he would puzzle over what to do. Sometimes he would say to a friend, "I couldn't sleep very well last night. Someone wants to borrow from me, and I'm not sure if lending money to him would be helping him out or helping him in."

While you are considering the other man, also consider yourself. If the money you are thinking of lending is all the money you have in the world, and if you are also doing the Lord's work and not getting paid much for it, you might want to lend your money where you at least get some interest. The apostle Paul would have said, "I mean not that other men be eased, and ye burdened" (2 Corinthians 8:13). Let other men shoulder the heavier financial burdens of the church if you cannot, while you serve the Lord in ways that they perhaps cannot. The ability to lend money is one of the gifts in the church, and not everyone has that gift.

Of course, if you are satisfied to see your money dwindle down to zero because you trust the Lord to provide for you at the zero-point, that is fine. But realize what you are doing. Once your money is gone, you will no longer be able to contribute as much to the brotherhood when major needs come up. In fact, you might have sudden needs—such as a doctor bill with which the church has to help *you*—that in earlier days you would have taken care of yourself. Be frank about this with yourself, with the Lord, and with one or two trustworthy advisers.

Once you have decided to lend, be definite with your terms. A young man once offered money to missions "for an indefinite period of time." They took this as a generous offer and accepted. A year or two later, he asked for the money back. This caused some awkwardness, and he is still embarrassed when he thinks of it. By "indefinite," he had simply meant he did not know when he would want it back. They probably thought of "indefinite" as a much longer period than it turned out to be. He and they could have prevented this misunderstanding by making the terms definite: "at least two years."

Now then, what about charging interest on a loan? At first glance, the Bible appears to condemn this. It frowns on "usury," and usury is interest. During the Middle Ages, the Roman

Catholic Church forbade its members to charge interest. That is one reason why many Jews became bankers. They could charge interest because they were not Catholics.

In the Bible's own words, "If thou lend money to any of my people that is poor by thee, thou shalt not be to him as an usurer, neither shalt thou lay upon him usury" (Exodus 22:25). Again, "If thy brother be waxen poor, and fallen in decay with thee; then thou shalt relieve him. . . . Take thou no usury of him. . . . Thou shalt not give him thy money upon usury, nor lend him thy victuals for increase" (Leviticus 25:35–37). Notice that these references speak specifically about lending to the poor.

Other Old Testament references to usury suggest the same thing—that the poor should get special consideration. In an interesting passage, Nehemiah commanded the nobles to restore to their struggling debtors "the hundredth part of the money" (Nehemiah 5:11). Translators are not sure of the exact meaning of this expression. It could refer to interest of one percent per month, which would be twelve percent per year.

How should we apply all this? When a struggling brother borrows to buy a car because he does not have the cash to buy it outright, an interest-free loan could be a good way to contribute to his need. On the other hand, when someone borrows money to make money (for example, to buy cows), it seems appropriate to require interest.[17]

Think of it this way. If you owned a farm and Brother Joe farmed it, you would normally charge rent. Now if you sold that farm to Brother Joe on a land contract, you would expect to charge interest on the unpaid balance. In this case, Brother Joe would be paying rent on the money you still have in the farm instead of on the farm itself.[18]

Naturally this does not answer all questions. What about someone who wants to buy a house but is not necessarily struggling financially? This falls between the two extremes we considered above. Probably you should get an idea of where the borrower is on the scale of

> *"Thou oughtest therefore to have put my money to the exchangers, and then at my coming I should have received mine own with usury"* (Matthew 25:27).

prosperity, and lend accordingly. Presumably, if you have money to lend, you are fairly high on the prosperity scale yourself and can afford to be fairly generous. In transactions between brothers, often the interest rate is better for the borrower than if he had borrowed in the business world, and better for the lender than if he had lent there.

When inflation runs high, the interest rate should be relatively high to compensate for it. A banker once made a remark something like this: "People reminisce to me about when they were getting eleven percent interest, and I say, 'No, you weren't. You were getting five percent because inflation was running at six percent.'"

But you cannot keep pace with everything. Sometimes you might deliberately allow inflation to outrun your interest rate because you want, in effect, to make a donation. In matters between Christian brothers, the rules of the high financial world do not always apply. There is only one rule: "Thou shalt love." All else is detail.

Charitable Trusts

What is a trust? James Smith used a very simple one when his son Samuel was earning his first paychecks. He put Samuel's money in a bank account "in trust for Samuel Smith." The money was Samuel's, but the control was the father's for a time, for he was more mature than his son.

Many trusts are more complicated than this, but they follow the same principle. The money or property is for "A," but it is under the control of "B." The person who sets up the trust (called a grantor) might choose to control it himself, or he might assign the management of it to someone else. The grantor might be a group rather than an individual, and the beneficiary might also be a group, such as a mission board.

Even if control were not an issue, taxes would be. Trusts can be managed in such a way as to reduce taxes, as you can see in the illustrations that follow.[19]

In the case of a charitable trust, the grantor places money

or property into a trust that holds it in behalf of a church or charitable organization. Why would a grantor do that instead of making an outright gift of his money?

First, he might have needs of his own and prefer to share his assets rather than giving them away. For example, he might want to continue receiving interest on his money or rent from a property as long as he lives, even though the money or property is given to the church. Or it might be the opposite: he wants to keep a property but give the income from it to the church. Often through arrangements like this, he can claim a charitable deduction from his income tax.

Suppose a retiring husband and wife want to sell a farm they bought many years ago for $50,000. The farm is now worth $200,000. Can they reduce the capital gains tax on the $150,000 difference? Yes. They can put $100,000 into a charitable trust, agreeing to accept interest on it as long as they live. When they die, the $100,000 will belong to the charitable organization.

Sometimes a person leaves money to the church or a mission in his will. This can be a considerable amount, which is good. But there is a downside. If a hundred thousand dollars suddenly shows up in the mission board's figures, people will look at it and decide they do not need to give very much because the mission is well taken care of. This is bad for their giving habits. It is bad for the mission, too, because moments will come when the mission board really does need a large amount of capital. If the board holds the money until it needs the capital, slackened giving in the meantime spells trouble.

The solution? The mission board can set up its own trust fund so people can will their money to it. The trust fund absorbs sudden influxes of capital. The fund trustees keep the figures private. They do not take money out of the fund for ordinary mission expenses. But if a new mission begins, or if a congregation needs help to build a new church, the money is there. The fund trustees might give a certain sum outright, or they might offer an interest-free loan.

Seven Principles for Sound Investment: A Summary

"One man's junk is another man's treasure." One customer barely glances at an old chest in the pawnshop because it is battered and full of wormholes. The next customer pays for it with trembling fingers because he considers it a valuable antique. One housewife throws out a pair of old work shoes. Another plants marigolds in them and sets them on the front porch!

Nowhere is disagreement over junk and treasure more evident than in the realm of investment. God and men see investment from totally opposite viewpoints. Humans think gain is godliness. The Bible says godliness is gain (1 Timothy 6:5, 6). Humans love this present world and invest in it. God's Word instructs us to invest in the world to come.

Strangely, the language God uses to set forth His principles sounds much the same as the language men use to describe theirs. You will notice this if you glance over the headings in this section. "Start early," "Have a system," "Invest in safe things," and so on. It sounds as if God and men are in total agreement! But the applications—that is where God and men differ drastically.

Here are seven sound principles along with sound applications.

Start early. In the world of finance, everyone knows that procrastination is expensive. If a twenty-five-year-old puts $150 monthly into an investment that pays 10 percent compound interest, by the time he reaches age 65, he will have over $900,000. If he starts at age 30, he will have over $500,000. If he starts at age 35, he will have over $300,000. If he starts at 45, he will have over $100,000. You see how the figure drops.

There is also a "cost of procrastination" in serving the Lord. With money? Yes, with money. Lay aside the question of compound interest—the Lord has His own way of figuring that! Simply think of it: the later you start giving to the Lord, the less the total amount you will give during your lifetime. It is an obvious fact.

Furthermore, the longer you postpone giving, the less inclined you will be to give much even when you do give. If you are out of the giving habit, getting into it will become harder, not easier. Even moderate giving will seem exorbitant.

Start young; and if it is appropriate in your setting, start your children young. When they go to church, giving should seem to them to be part of the worship experience—for so it is.

Start early, but do not be discouraged if you started late. If someone is fifty years old before he starts saving money, would his banker advise him to just forget about saving money? No; rather, he should do what he can while he can.

Someone who has newly given his heart to the Lord in midlife or old age will rightly regret all the money he squandered on himself over the years. If that is your case, do not waste an undue amount of time in regret. Most successful people—yes, Bible heroes—had regrets. The apostle Paul as a young man wasted his time and resources on persecuting Christians. But that just made him all the more determined to serve the Lord with whatever resources he had left at the time of his conversion.

Have a system. Government officials know the value of being systematic in investment and how hard it is for many people to have a system. So they obligate people to give a certain amount from their paychecks so they can get it back when they are old. Citizens question whether that arrangement will work in the long run, but we must at least give government leaders credit for one thing—they believe in having a system.

Old Testament saints were also required to have a system of investment, though it was called "offerings." Exodus, Leviticus, and Numbers give many details about animal sacrifices—what to do with the blood, the fat, and the rest of the sacrifice (see Exodus 29:11–14). Having it all spelled out did not spoil the fact that it would be a "sweet savour" to the Lord (Exodus 29:18).

God also directed the Israelites on how to invest in their poor neighbors. "If thy brother be waxen poor, and hath sold away some of his possession . . ." (Leviticus 25:25). The passage goes on to explain in detail how to help their neighbors. Once again, this was a way of investing in relationships with God and men

137

which would have great rewards.

These New Testament days, we should know how to be systematic without being told in such detail. When the offering plate is passed, we should know better than to simply reach into a pocket and pull out whatever we find there. Rather, we should calculate the Lord's due with all deliberate speed when we get our paycheck.

The apostle Paul would say amen to this, judging from his directions to one of the churches. "Upon the first day of the week let every one of you lay by him in store, as God hath prospered him, that there be no gatherings when I come" (1 Corinthians 16:2).

Have a system—but be flexible. People find that during some periods of their lives, they are able to save more for investment purposes. Other times, they are able to save less—or perhaps nothing at all.

Similarly, when you are young, you can devote more time and money directly to the work of the church. After you have a family, you spend proportionately more time serving the Lord by raising your family (not that you fail to support the church). When you get old, things will be somewhat different again.

In any case, do not be so systematic that you actually hinder the Lord's work. Even in Old Testament times, people were encouraged to do more than their fair share. How much more should that be today! Never come to the point where you say, "Here's the cutoff line, even though I could do more. I've done my part now." That's being *too* systematic. Jesus taught His followers to go the second mile, which means going above and beyond the call of system.

Invest in safe things. Sensible investors put their money into operations they understand and trust rather than into junk bonds. True, the shaky enterprises offer a higher rate of interest, but that is because they have to—they are shaky. Quite possibly the investor will get nothing for his investment. He might even lose the investment itself.

How did Jesus apply that principle to us? "Lay not up for yourselves treasures upon earth, where moth and rust doth corrupt, and where thieves break through and steal: but lay up for yourselves treasures in heaven, where neither moth nor rust doth corrupt, and where thieves do not break through nor steal" (Matthew 6:19, 20).

A child's song puts it this way.

> There's a place of sure deposit,
>> Kept safe by God's own seal,
> Where moth and rust doth not corrupt,
>> Nor thieves break through and steal;
> So in that bank of heaven,
>> My treasures I will store,
> And I'll find them all awaiting me
>> When I reach that happy shore.[20]

Invest in safe things—but accept some risk. Investors in this world's goods know that there is no such thing as zero risk. They speak of one's "sleep threshold"—how much risk one can accept and still sleep. Some people can take on more risk, some less.

The one-talent servant of Matthew 25 thought he would play it safe. He buried his talent so he would not lose it. In the end he lost it anyway—not just his talent but everything he had. If he had been frightened into action instead of inaction, he would actually have risked less rather than more.

Diversify. Do not put all your eggs into one basket. Investors put their money into various interests. If one place fails to produce money, hopefully another will do extra well to make up for it.

There is a practical lesson for us in this. We ought to invest in more than one narrow interest. Yes, that one narrow interest might be good—our own family, for instance. But some people focus on their families to the exclusion of other healthy interests. Sooner or later, they discover that their children grow up and marry into other families that it would have been wise to take an interest in all along.

Diversify—but not too much. A real estate man might diversify his interests but still prefer to keep them within the realm of real estate. He does not invest in shipping or mining, where he knows little.

Christians may have many interests, but they must always keep Christ at the center. "My business is serving the Lord," said one brother. "I farm to pay the bills." He was first a Christian and then a farmer. If we involve ourselves in too many projects, we might not do any of them well.

Invest where the returns are good. That is what people of the world try to do. If an investment is not profitable, they free themselves of it and try something else.

Does a Christian receive good returns on his investment? Certainly, and not all of them are out of this world. Many returns for serving the Lord are *in* this world, rewards that cannot be measured by money. For example, consider the reward of knowing that our sacrifices for the Lord mean something to the Lord. For another example, consider the reward of investing in young people and seeing them blossom into fruitful adults.

What about practical investment advice? What returns are best? Much of the answer depends on how we measure. If all we want in returns is dollars and cents, predictions of a hot, dry summer would indicate that it is better to invest in beer companies.

Not interested? Why not? Because you want your money to do some good while it is generating money. Why not use that same yardstick to measure other investments? That is, where can your money do some good while it is working for you?

What about investing in Coca-Cola? The drink quenches the thirst without intoxicating the drinker. Besides, it gives him a little energy in the form of sugar and caffeine. "Things go better with Coke," they tell us. Maybe so.

However instead of asking, "Where can my money do some good?" we should be asking, "What would the Lord have us do with our money?" We have only a short time in all eternity to do this; why not do it right?

That is the reason to put a big question mark on investing in mutual funds. Some people are troubled by the unequal yoke involvements in mutual funds, and that is a valid concern. But perhaps an even greater question is, Why not invest in something that gives a much greater return?

Why not invest in Christian publishers, for instance? What about helping the brother who is starting in business? How about the farmers who recently moved to another state and are having a difficult time? Have you thought of the brother-in-law who wants to buy a house?

> *"A hundred years from now it will not matter much if my bank account was large or small, but the world may be different because I was important in the life of a child."*

Some of these investments might offer a fair rate of interest; others might not. There are a number of things to consider in any such decision. But while you are considering everything else, consider this question: What is my money doing besides generating income?

Invest where returns are good—but remember that small causes can have good returns. Businessmen who "think big" sometimes make out well, but sometimes they wish they had never expanded. They were just as prosperous, with fewer headaches, before the expansion. Business arithmetic can play strange tricks.

In the kingdom of God too, strange things take place. Two mites are worth more than hundreds of dollars. A cup of cold water given in one world receives its reward in the next. The story of one selfless act gets told around the world.

Jesus could think small. He did not always preach to masses. Sometimes He sat down to talk with one person, like Nicodemus. He was not too busy to bless little children.

Stick to your investment. In the secular world, people are learning this. They find that it often does not pay to make short-term investments, because they are liable to jump in and out of the market at the wrong time. The key, they say, is to keep their money invested.

There is a spiritual application. "Be patient therefore, brethren, unto the coming of the Lord" (James 5:7). "And let us not be weary in well doing: for in due season we shall reap, if we faint not" (Galatians 6:9).

Stick to your investment, but cut your losses when necessary. A woman was troubled when visitors pointed out that her television was doing her soul no good. But she had spent money to buy the television. "If I got rid of it," she said, "all that money would be lost." Her visitors replied, "That money was lost the day you bought the television." She was trying to hold on to money she no longer had. She had nothing to lose.

> Do not go along with the crowd. Good investors buy when the crowd is selling and sell when the crowd is buying. It takes courage. That is exactly what the Christian is supposed to do. He chooses an investment that is not popular, believes in his investment, and stays invested.

If a project you thought was a good one does not hold out, it is perfectly all right to give it up. Find something better to do. The producer of *The Living Bible,* according to his own account, once attempted to generate more income for his family by trying to make some fast profits in the stock market. He bought a number of stocks that were supposed to shoot up in value. Whenever his broker would call and give him a hot tip, he would buy. But the day came when his broker said, "Of my hundreds of customers, you are the only one who lost money last year!" The man got out.[21]

Make friends with your money. In the world of high finance, how many people do make friends? Rather, the game seems to be, "Sell at the right time, and let someone else bear the loss."

However, even among ungodly people, there is a saying, "What goes around comes around." Generous people are well liked, and their generosity often comes back to them.

Jesus put it this way: "Make to yourselves friends of the mammon of unrighteousness; that, when ye fail, they may receive you into everlasting habitations" (Luke 16:9). In other words, use earthly riches wisely to make heavenly friends.

Make friends with your money—but expect to make some enemies too. At least expect some people to disapprove. A young man in the service of the Lord met a former teacher, who took him aside and said, "Now look here . . . we thought a good deal of you, and we had hopes that you would achieve something great. Do you mean to tell me that this is what you are?"[22]

Jesus' disciples, especially Judas, disapproved of Mary's sacrifice. "Why this waste?" they wondered (Mark 14:4; John 12:5). Judas thought he knew better how to handle money, only to fling money away from himself—literally—a few days later. A sinner considers a Christian's investment to be a waste. Don't worry; it is not.

Jesus approved of what Mary had done. What better return could one wish for? Money cannot buy His friendship, yet money has something to do with it. Handling money in ways He approves will heighten His commendation on our lives when we finally meet Him.

Jesus is more than a friend. He is an astute financial adviser. The rich young ruler apparently never heard Jesus say, "Thou shalt have treasure in heaven." Yet after he walked away, Jesus re-emphasized it: "an hundredfold now in this time . . . and in the world to come eternal life" (Mark 10:30).

> *Did Jesus make a unique demand of the rich young ruler? Not at all, as Peter immediately pointed out. "Lo, we have left all, and have followed thee" (Mark 10:28).*

He offered 100-fold; that is, 10,000 percent interest for a lifetime of serving the Lord. Of course, He did not mean to be held to the exact dollar. He did mean, however, that He was perfectly, literally serious when He told the rich young ruler, "Thou shalt have treasure in heaven." He is perfectly serious today. He says it to you and me: "Take my investment advice, and you *shall* have treasure in heaven."

Retirement

As Christians, we have a concept of retirement that is entirely different from the world's.

In the first place, we do not retire. We try to stay as productive as we can for as long we can. True, a farmer might sell his farm, but then he will drop in on his son's or friend's farm and help where he can. A "retired" painter or carpenter who must stay off tall ladders will nevertheless find porches to paint, pictures to hang, and chairs to reglue.

In the second place, we know a God that the world does not know. Our security is not in things but in Him. Just as we lock our doors at night and trust God for the rest, we save something for old age if we can and trust God for the rest. "I have been young, and now am old; yet have I not seen the righteous forsaken, nor his seed begging bread" (Psalm 37:25).

"Unplanned retirement can be fatal. A patient came to see me, rubbing his hands together. 'I'm retiring in June.'

" 'Oh, and what are you going to do?'

" 'Well, I'll paint the house, and there are all sorts of repairs about the place that I've wanted to do for years.'

" 'And then?'

" 'Oh, I don't know . . .'

"He was dead in a year. Again and again this happened. I did not retire."[23]

In the third place, we follow a frugal lifestyle that the world does not want. Books about finances talk about maintaining one's lifestyle through retirement. But the authors are visualizing a cottage by the lake, boats, new cars, and extensive travel. Our lifestyle includes family, friends, and church. These give us good reasons for living, along with sources of diversion—basically all the values we want—without a costly price tag.

Several hundred years ago, the line between God's people and the world was not so clearly marked as today. Most people belonged to an *extended* family, with grandparents, aunts, uncles, and cousins living near each other and helping each other. Always there were people in the group too young or too old to work much, but always there were people who could work to support them all.

Then came the Industrial Revolution. The able-bodied went to factories to work, and those who could not work stayed home. As time went on and transportation to distant areas became more common, people went to where the work was, rather than staying where their extended family was. A new sense of family developed—the concept of the *nuclear* family; that is, a nucleus consisting of a father, a mother, and their children.

Of course, this change did not happen overnight. The population remained rural for a long time. Farm families often had a little house next to the big house, where Grandpa and Grandma lived. Grandpa could still putter around the property, doing what he could and resting when he got tired.

Still, preparing for old age became more and more one's own responsibility. Some people did well at taking care of their own needs, and some did not. Seeing this problem, various planners came forward with programs to help make old age more secure

Although our older people do not find old age as troublesome as some might expect, they do have their problems. They must make adjustments at a time of life when adjustments come hard. Friends they once counted on are getting old themselves. Getting rid of property means getting rid of the headaches of upkeep, but it also means that their property no longer gives them an income or puts a roof over their heads. They no longer need to feed a family, but they might need to pay more doctor bills. We have to face these facts realistically.

and comfortable.

Members of religious groups who practiced a separated lifestyle diverged from the world in this matter and in many cases did not fully realize how different from the community they were becoming. But society's retirement programs could hardly fail to escape their attention. They began to wonder how involved they should be in these programs.

Life Insurance Annuities

We often think of life insurance in terms of a death. If you die insured, the company pays a sum of money to your survivors. But life insurance has other features too, including retirement plans. Life insurance companies provide periodic payments, called annuities, to retired people who have bought into their programs.

From a financial viewpoint, is the retirement aspect of life insurance a good idea? There are better ideas. If you took the same amount of money and invested it in a savings account, allowing it to accumulate compound interest, you would likely come out ahead over the years.

Having an insurance policy is like banking in reverse. A bank will pay you a little for your savings, but an insurance company will expect you to pay for the privilege of saving with them. A bank lets you take your own money out of your own savings account without charge (at certain intervals), but an insurance company will charge you a low rate of interest to let you use your own money. And all this has not even mentioned the dampening effect that life insurance has on one's concept of God's providence. Keep on reading!

Social Security

Governments of industrialized nations have seen how tragically poverty-stricken many people become in old age. The authorities naturally want to offer assistance. That assistance came to the United States during Franklin D. Roosevelt's administration, in the form of the Social Security Act. Canada has a similar plan called Social Insurance.

Basically, social security is an enforced savings plan. The government makes sure the worker saves some money for old age by saving it for him. Every time he gets his paycheck, a certain amount of it is skimmed off and sent to the Department of the Treasury.[24] The employer matches the worker's contribution; in other words, if the worker pays a hundred dollars, the employer also pays a hundred.

Can the worker watch his pile accumulate? In one way he can, because the government sends him a statement about it every so often. In another way he cannot, because the government uses his money to pay retired people who are already receiving social security payments. When the worker himself reaches retirement age, the theory goes, he will receive money out of payments that younger workers are making.

It is common knowledge that people depending on social security are worried. At this writing, many millions of future social security recipients are already turning gray at their temples. How will the social security program manage to pay them all as they retire and the work force shrinks? Social security is not all that secure.

If a person objects on religious grounds to receiving social security payments, he may apply for a Form 4029 exemption from

What about the retired brother who is well established financially but also draws social security payments so he has plenty of money to give to the Lord's work?

Even Christians who do not reject social security in principle raise their eyebrows at this. Remember, the government gets its money from taxpayers. Social security money going to this brother has come out of many working people's pockets. He is not so generous as he thinks he is.

making payments into the social security fund. However, there are a few conditions attached, as indicated on the application below. Then too, the government might not accept the claim of a person who belongs to a newly formed independent church with no history of objection to social security.

Form 4029: Application for Exemption From Social Security and Medicare Taxes and Waiver of Benefits

I certify that I am and continuously have been a member of (Name of religious group, Religious district and location) since (Month, Day, and Year) and as a follower of the established teachings of that group, I am conscientiously opposed to accepting benefits of any private or public insurance . . .

I waive all rights to any social security payment or benefit . . .

A writer also makes the following interesting observation.

The United States government has given us the privilege of being social security exempt. The present social security rate of 13 percent gives the exempt earner with $20,000 per year $2,600 more in income than one who is not exempt. If the average church has 30 members who contribute regularly, this exemption gives its membership a total savings of $78,000. The average mission is being financed by five churches, so the potential pool of social security savings becomes $390,000. . . . If our incomes stayed the same but we lost our social security exemption, we would still have enough to live on. What happens to this extra money every year? . . .

. . . I do not advocate that all extra money go to the mission fields, or any other good cause. However, this does give us a glimpse of what we could do and helps us see the importance of using our money rightly.[25]

The figures above assume the taxpayer is self-employed. A wage earner would save half this amount.

Company Pension Plans

The government likes to see people comfortable in their retirement, so it offers tax benefits to companies that save on behalf of their employees. Some companies save by contributing regularly to a trust fund in a bank,[26] or to an insurance company.[27]

Others invest in stocks—perhaps their own. When a worker finally retires, his company dips into this fund and gives him a stipend (regular payment). In some cases the employee may also contribute to the fund. The 401(k) plan is an example of this.

Some companies have a system called profit sharing. The rate at which it grows depends on the company's profits.

Are company pension plans safe? Well, underfunded pension plans are not unheard of. And even if the money is there, it is invested somewhere—perhaps in common stocks that can go down as easily as up.

Many companies insure their plans with the Pension Benefit Guaranty Corporation,[28] which is supposed to solve any problems. However, this company is itself capable of running a deficit and has already done so.[29]

Individual Pension Plans

IRA stands for Individual Retirement Account. Its counterpart in Canada is RRSP—Registered Retirement Savings Plan. Either plan offers a tax break to people who do their own saving for retirement. One option is the traditional IRA, in which your money is exempt from income tax until you withdraw it; but once you are old enough to do that, the tax will presumably be lower because you will be in a lower tax bracket. Another option is the Roth IRA, with which no tax deduction is allowed now but all the income generated by the fund is exempt from future taxation. This is an advantage if you will be in a higher tax bracket in old age.

Having a tax-sheltered retirement fund is no small matter.

When Joseph is twenty years old, he begins investing a tenth of his $30,000 annual income in a traditional IRA. That is $3,000 each year. He does this by depositing $250 per month for forty years, until he is sixty years old, and receives 6 percent interest compounded monthly. How much does he have at age 60?

Obtaining the final amount is a complex procedure. Suffice it to say that Joseph would have about $497,870 by age 60. (You can verify this by multiplying $250 × 1.005 to obtain the balance after the first month. Add $250; then multiply the sum by 1.005 to obtain the balance after the second month. Follow these steps 480 times because there are 480 months in forty years.)

Joseph's sister Geraldine also earns $30,000 a year, and she also invests $250 per month ($3,000 per year). But she does not use a tax-sheltered account. This means she must pay tax, first of all, on all $30,000 instead of on $27,000, as Joseph does. Did I say she has $3,000 to invest? Excuse me, income tax has neatly removed a sizable amount of that—let us say a thousand dollars—leaving her $2,000 to invest.

Once again, we must figure taxes. Once again, they take a neat bite, not only out of what Geraldine is investing but also out of the interest she earns on that investment. Once again, we will assume taxes take a third. So in effect, Geraldine is not really earning 6 percent interest; she is earning 4 percent. In forty years, she will have about $295,490. The difference between Joseph's and Geraldine's savings is—well, I'll let you do the subtracting.

Let us try again with more-modest figures. Suppose Joseph and Geraldine both earn $24,000 a year. In this case, Joseph would save $2,400 a year tax-free, on 6 percent interest, and have $398,300 in the end. Geraldine would save $1,600 a year after taxes, on 4 percent interest after taxes, and get $157,590. This is theoretical, of course, and other factors enter in. But it shows the potential we are looking at.

Is an IRA safe? That largely depends on your choices. You can have your IRA money go into a conservative account with fixed interest rates. This is safe, but your savings will not grow very fast. You can have your money

> *Of course, there is always someone around who argues that social security shortfalls may become so acute that the government will consider taxing IRAs after all.[30]*

go into a liberal account, which means your IRA manager will invest it in stocks. Over a period of thirty or forty years, you will probably come out ahead, if history is any indication. You can invest in something in between, which means mutual funds.

Is the money you have invested in an IRA doing what you want it to be doing? A large sum of money is a powerful thing. The people who hold your IRA money will be using it for something—good, bad, or neutral. The businesses your IRA money supports will be secular—in other words, neutral at best. Car manufacturers, telephone companies, chemical companies, appliance makers, and airlines would be illustrations.

One might argue that we do put money in the bank without asking questions about what the bank does with it. But the bank holds it for a relatively short time, and we do not have much choice but to do our banking at the bank. With long-term investing, however, we have more options and more accountability.

Keep Christ and His kingdom in focus. You want to hear, "Well done, thou good and faithful servant: . . . enter thou into the joy of thy Lord" (Matthew 25:21).

Church

Have churches, like other institutions, moved into the field of retirement investment? Some of them have. The back cover of a Lutheran magazine carries an ad that says, "We've been helping people link their faith, values, and finances for more than 80 years. See your local Lutheran Brotherhood district representative." A Lutheran Brotherhood representative confirmed that they offer retirement plans, and he said other denominations do too.

What about our own conservative churches? We members stick together. It is not enough for us to worship together; we want to draw together in other ways too. Our conservative lifestyle and manner of dress help us to do this. Finding our financial security among our own people also helps us to do it.

This is especially obvious in the case of accidents and hospital bills. The deacons in our churches definitely help here, and the whole arrangement is good for the giver as well as the receiver.

However, our churches do not provide for members in their old age as readily as if they had an accident or a large hospital bill. There might be several reasons for this. For one thing, people should know that in the normal course of life, they will get old. So why should they not prepare for this in one way or another? People whom God has given nothing to save should not consider themselves sinners because they are not saving. But if they have the ability to make arrangements for themselves, and through shortsightedness they fail to get it done, that is a different matter.

Family

By now we have come full circle, and we are back to family again. The Bible makes families responsible for their old people. It says that the young should "requite their parents" (1 Timothy 5:4) and "let not the church be charged" (verse 16), except for elderly people who have no family (verse 3).

It was easier to do this several generations ago than it is today (at least from our perspective). Back then, Father and Mother did not move far away when they got old. Father, who was now Grandpa, could still work about the farm as he felt able, slowing down more and more as the years went by. All the while, he and Grandma felt secure in knowing they were close to the family and would be supported even after they were no longer productive.

These days it is different, though not so different as people might think. Adult children are still responsible to provide some economic security for their elderly parents. Ideally, that should include an offer of a home with one of the children rather than sending Grandpa or Grandma to an old people's home.*

Jesus' own example gives one answer to providing for parents. Since His mother was apparently a widow and He was her eldest son, the burden of providing for His mother must have fallen mainly on His shoulders. Yet during His ministry, Jesus was evidently penniless. How He provided for His mother in life, we do not know. But when He was dying, He disposed of the problem by saying, "Woman, behold thy son!" And to John, "the disciple whom Jesus loved," Jesus said, "Behold thy mother!" (John 19:26, 27). The Bible adds, "And from that hour that disciple took her unto his own home." Our Lord's answer was not a bank account but friends.

It is interesting that Jesus did not give that responsibility to his

---

* This may vary. In some cases the elderly parents prefer to go to an old people's home.

blood brothers, who were out of sympathy with Him at the time. He found someone outside His immediate family, as many of us must do. Although the rule in looking for financial help should be "first family, then church," there are many variations on this. Our financial security lies with friends who stick closer than brothers.

A Revolutionary Concept

Some Christians deliberately choose not to save for retirement. They argue that this amounts to laying up treasure on earth, which Jesus condemned. One brother wondered what would happen if every thirty-year-old son would go to his sixty-year-old father and encourage him to give away his retirement savings, promising to support him in his old age.

There are several appealing things about this approach.

- It avoids taking the Lord's money out of circulation. This stands in contrast to money in an IRA that goes to support something either neutral or negative rather than serving the cause of the Gospel.
- In terms of laying up treasure in heaven, it is a no-risk proposition. Retirement savings involve so much money held in reserve over such a long time that the risk of loss is rather high, even in "secure" North America. Throughout history, people have lost their life savings in various ways, in some cases losing treasure in heaven that they could have had if they had given it to the Lord's work.
- Friends and family are more secure than money. A pile of money can leave without saying good-bye. Friends and family will do what they can for you, even if they cannot do much.

On the other hand, if a person saves nothing for his old age on the principle that he should give his assets away, he needs to consider several questions.

- How do his beliefs affect the way he presently treats his parents (and his wife's parents)? Is he supporting them in the way he expects to be supported?
- Is he giving to the Lord's cause the amount he would save

if he did save for old age? If he is spending all his money on present needs and wants, he is probably not living up to the spirit of his profession.

- Does he have an understanding with his children, or with anyone else, that he expects to be supported in his old age? Even one's own children do not like to be taken by surprise. Remember too that whereas the Bible says that children should "requite their parents" (1 Timothy 5:4), it also says "the children ought not to lay up for the parents, but the parents for the children" (2 Corinthians 12:14). Parents should do their part long before they expect children to do theirs.
- If he has no children able to support him, does he expect the church to do it? Most churches want to know this ahead of time, since most churches are not in the business of supporting old people!
- If he simply plans to go it alone, depending on the Lord and not asking anyone for anything, does he practice living that way now? Some people do live that way, and no doubt the Lord will provide for them when they get old just as He has been doing all along. But people who bump along, expecting vaguely that something will turn up at the end of the road, might be seriously disappointed.

In Conclusion

Obviously, the way we think about retirement will affect what we do about it. The reverse is also true—what we do about retirement will affect the way we think. If we take part in worldly programs, we will end up thinking in worldly terms. If we follow Bible principles, we will be paving the way for our own clear thinking, and for our children's as well.

5. Borrowing

A young man energetically swung his ax, then looked in horror. The axhead had slipped from the handle! Mercifully, the head did not hit anyone working nearby, but (small comfort!) it splashed into a nearby river and disappeared.

Getting the attention of his supervisor, the young man said, "Alas, master! for it was borrowed" (2 Kings 6:5). Whatever we may think of his chopping technique, he had the right concept of borrowing. He was responsible to return the whole ax to the lender.

Borrowing and lending still go on today, and the same principle applies. The borrower is responsible to the lender. In fact, the Bible flatly says, "The borrower is servant to the lender" (Proverbs 22:7).

These days we do not always use the words *lend* or *borrow*. We also use terms like *charge* and *credit*. The terms may be new, but they deal with what is basically an old subject.

Frankly, this is what I plan to say in this chapter.
- Business debt is acceptable within reason.
- Property debt is slightly less desirable, being dubious as an investment. (See the chapter on investments.) Still, many people borrow to purchase their own homes.
- Automobile debt is to be shunned at almost any cost.
- Consumer debt opens the door to a fool's paradise.

In summary,

"Credit can be a useful tool or a cruel master."

Business Debt

Debt can jump-start a business. For a simple example, think of a grocery store just starting up. The owner does not have enough capital to buy the groceries he needs. So he borrows enough to buy the groceries, sells them to customers, and pays back the loan. Without debt, there would be no grocery store.

Putting it another way, borrowing solves the problem suggested in the old saying, "You need money to make money." Some people scoff at this idea, but it often holds true. Suppose you want to buy a logging truck. Without money you cannot buy the truck, and without the truck you cannot make money. What do you do? You borrow money, buy the truck, and then use the truck to make more money than you borrowed.

Who benefits? Not just you. All the workers who helped to assemble the truck make money, which they would not have done if you had not borrowed money. The sawmill workers make money cutting up the logs into lumber. The lumber store makes money. The carpenters who buy the lumber to build and sell houses make money.

The bankers obviously benefit too, but so do the people who deposited money in the bank to make it possible for you to borrow it. The interest you pay is not wasted, not at all. Some of it goes into the pockets of people who buy houses made from lumber made from logs hauled by *your* logging truck. So some of the interest you pay ends up in your own pocket. (The circle might not be that small and simple, but this illustrates how the system works.) No wonder it seems that everyone is encouraging you to borrow.

On a smaller scale but coming in the same category is a business charge account. Businesses have things to do other than making many small payments at stores where they make many purchases. Receiving a statement at the end of the month and paying a lump sum (on time) saves time.

How much may you borrow? It depends on how much money you already have and how much you can reasonably expect to earn. Even if you are not buying a farm, the following quotation might shed a bit of light. "An old reliable standard for borrowing was that one should possess one-half of what was required to purchase a farm. With the inventory of cattle and equipment needed to operate a profitable enterprise today, this requirement may possibly be adjusted. If all the cattle and machinery are paid for and one has 25 to 33 percent of the purchase price, it may be safe to purchase a farm if reasonable interest can be obtained."[2]

Of course, the smaller the debt, the better. Avoid borrowing all you dare. If a debt is too big, it preoccupies the mind and depresses the spirit. What is bad for the mind is bad for the soul as well. A big debt also occupies a man's time so much that he has little left over for church work, let alone being free to serve in a foreign mission.

Furthermore, if the borrower gets into a tight spot, he will be sorely tempted by government programs that promise to bail him out of his dollar problems. This gives him a different perception of providence than if he worked his way out with the help of God's people.

We hear that businessmen sometimes become much too self-permissive about debts. Some are in up to their ears, hoping the economy keeps on booming. If it does not, they are in trouble.

One writer asks pointedly, "Is it not ironical that a group of Christian people . . . used to being self-employed in smaller businesses, basically farm or rural, should, through a time of booming prosperity, regress from a community largely self-supporting with a pay-as-you-go policy, to a community operating largely on borrowed capital? We have become poorer, rather than richer, even while we say, as the Laodiceans, 'I am rich, and increased with goods.' We just think we are!"[3]

George Müller wrote, "Another reason why children of God do not succeed in their calling is that they try to begin their business with too little capital. If a believer has no capital at all, or very little capital in comparison with what his business requires, he should ask himself, 'If it is my heavenly Father's will that I begin this business, He would have given me the money I need to get started. And since He has not, is this a plain indication that for now I should remain at my present job?'"[4]

We look with disapproval upon people who, just prior to the Great Depression, borrowed money to invest in stocks. When the market collapsed, they all tried to get their hands out of the cookie jar at once, and many of them could not. But are we much better than they if we run ourselves seriously in debt to finance our own businesses? If the business goes poorly, will we have any way to escape, or will we be totally stuck?

Property Debt

Bankers are much more free about lending money than they used to be. Gone are the days when you walked tremblingly into a bank and had to explain in detail to a frowning officer why you needed a loan, and why you believed you could pay it back in time. Bankers have learned that the risk of having a customer default on his loan is usually less than the 100 percent certainty of getting nothing if they never make the loan. So today you have to serve as your own frowning officer.

Of course, the creditors will have some questions. They want to know if you are a good manager and a steady person. How long have you been working at your present job? What kind of income do you have? Do you have any savings? Are you presently in debt, and for how much and how long?

> "If you don't get the facts, the facts will get you."[5]

A debt on a house or property usually takes the form of a mortgage. This agreement gives the bank or other creditor the right to foreclose if a borrower cannot make his payments. The bank takes possession of the property and sells it in order to get the money back.

Mortgages are expensive, as even banks admit. One bank manager told about his wife's reaction when she found out the total amount they would have to pay for their home, including interest. "She jumped right out of her chair, and I had to put her back in again."

Why so costly? A key word here is *amortization*, the process of "killing" a large debt by making regular payments. Suppose you buy a house with a mortgage of $100,000. Paying $300 every month would get the house paid off neatly in twenty-five years. There is one catch, however—you also have to pay interest. At an annual interest rate of 8½ percent, the interest on $100,000 is more than $700 the first month! If you hope to pay off the house, your monthly payment must be more than that.

According to an amortization table, a monthly payment of $805.22 will pay off the loan and interest in twenty-five years. The first month, less than $100 of that goes to pay off the principal. The interest payment will be slightly less the next month because you have reduced the debt by almost $100. This means that a slightly larger fraction of your payment will go toward reducing the principal. Over the years, this fraction will grow larger and larger, and the portion going toward interest will be smaller and smaller. By

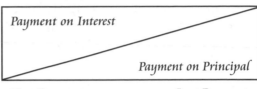

the twenty-fourth year, practically all of your payment will go toward reducing the mortgage balance. The graph above shows that as you move from left to right, the total payment remains the same but the proportion changes.

The following table gives actual figures to show how this works for the first three and last three payments.

Payment	Principal	Interest	Balance
1	96.89	708.33	99,903.11
2	97.58	707.65	99,805.53
3	98.27	706.96	99,707.25
298	788.36	16.87	1,593.50
299	793.94	11.29	799.56
300	799.56	5.66	0.00

Finally you will own the house free and clear, and you can stop making payments. But in the meantime, how much will you have spent? Multiply the payment of $805.22 by the three hundred months in twenty-five years, and you come up with $241,566. That is more than twice the $100,000 originally borrowed. Yes, you can take comfort in the thought that other people benefited from all the money you paid. But you have other demands on your money, and you must take a responsible attitude toward your finances.

Here are several principles relating to property debt.

- You can normally buy a house two and a half times the value of your annual before-tax income. At least, this is what experts used to say. They are more cautious now, considering all the costs of home ownership.[6]
- Monthly payments plus property taxes should not be more than 30 percent of your monthly gross income. All other debts should not bring the total to more than 40 percent.[7]
- You should be able to make a 25 percent down payment.[8]

Is there anything you can do to reduce the interest you must pay?

Reduce the principal, of course. Buy a more modest property than you would have preferred. Buy a house that needs freshening up, and ask friends to come for a few Saturday work bees. Build a small house that you can expand later.

See if you can shorten the amortization period. The payments will be bigger, but you can save quite a bit of interest. In fact, the bank may recommend this for your own good.

See if you can get a better deal than the bank gives you, at least for part of the mortgage. Maybe your uncle or brother-in-law can help you out. If you end up owing several sources, pay off the most expensive one first, which is probably the bank.

We noted elsewhere that it is a good idea to lend within the brotherhood. For equally obvious reasons, it is a good idea to borrow there. Just as lending to a brother at a reasonable interest rate benefits him, so borrowing from him at a reasonable interest rate also benefits him. It feels satisfying, when money leaves your hands, to know that it is doing the Lord's people some good.

Vehicle Debt

As previously noted, it may be justifiable for a business to go into debt to buy a vehicle like a logging truck. But borrowing to buy a personal vehicle—there is a problem.

Borrowing to buy a new car is especially fraught with dangers.

Hardly anything in the business world is more unpleasant than paying for a car that is no longer worth the payments, which will probably be true by the time of the fiftieth payment some four years down the road.

Well, *one* thing is more unpleasant—having the car repossessed by the lender. Some creditors even repossess cars in the dead of night. The debtor wakes up in the morning to find that his car is gone. No fuss, no muss.

It is much more pleasant to drive a rattletrap.

Consumer Debt

"Can I help you?" a polite-voiced airport ticket agent asked Robert.

"Yes," said Robert. "I'm trying to obtain my boarding pass electronically, but this device doesn't seem able to identify my credit card."

"May I see your ticket, please? Hmm. Mr. Anderson, this ticket isn't for tonight at all. It's for the twenty-third. That's a week from today." The agent handed the ticket back to Robert, who stared at it. The agent was right, and Robert was dead wrong. Yes, he had come to the airport at the right time, but he had confused the dates when ordering the ticket.

"Let me step back and think about this," Robert said to the agent, picking up his luggage. Finding a quiet corner, Robert pondered his situation. It was just after midnight. A friend had dropped him off at the curb ten minutes ago and was now on his way home, some sixty miles away. In any case, Robert could not honorably go home again because he had an appointment nearly a continent away that very evening, and two more the next day.

Reluctantly, Robert reached for his wallet. His ticket for next week was nonrefundable, so the money was lost—unless he had an emergency next week at just the right time to justify his flying again! There was nothing he could do but buy a new ticket. On such short notice, it would be expensive.

On his credit card, of course. This would give him until the end of the month to juggle his finances and get his new debt paid for.

This little story illustrates three reasons why some people justify the use of credit cards: (1) identification, (2) traveling, and (3) emergencies.

However, individuals use credit cards and other forms of consumer credit much less often for emergencies than for convenience. Rather than paying for a purchase every time he runs to his favorite store, a customer can say, "Charge it." The store records his purchases in his charge account and sends him a monthly statement. He pays for all his purchases at once.

Buying on credit has become a way of life. In fact, some businesses assume that you want it. (Why not?) If you do business with them long enough, they will notify you that now, as a valued business customer, you have an account with them.

Not content with that, businesses have made things even more convenient for the customer. He need not pay in full at the end of the month. He can put off the payment, or pay only in part. This makes payments easier for the time being. Of course, he has to pay interest for the privilege.

Getting a credit card is very easy. Just ask your local bank. To make it even easier, you get occasional offers in your mailbox from credit card companies—perhaps even with a credit card enclosed. If you want to use the card, fill out a form and send it in.

> Credit is *"an attractive name for consumer debt."*

Once the card is activated, you can walk into a store and buy anything you see. Just hand the cashier your credit card instead of money. She swipes it in a device that instantly makes a phone call to the credit card company to check your credit limit. The company computer approves your purchase up to a limit of perhaps two or three thousand dollars, and all you have to do is sign your name. Once you have made a number of such purchases and paid them off, proving that you can be trusted, the company will consider raising your credit limit.

Having credit means you need not worry about carrying enough cash with you. You can shop the day before your paycheck arrives rather than making two trips—one to buy absolute necessities with your last twenty-dollar bill, and the other to buy everything else you need once the money comes.

Using a credit card is a painless way to shop. You feel no sense of loss, because the cashier gives the card back to you along with a receipt.

> *"High prices don't bother me anymore. My credit card pays for everything now."*

Then your wallet is fuller than it was before.

So credit is handy for a buyer. What value is there in the credit system for stores and businesses?

Obviously, they get more business from customers who like convenience. The following list is from a leaflet that encourages merchants to let their customers pay with credit cards.

FIVE REASONS TO ACCEPT CARDS

Increase sales. Customers spend incrementally more per ticket and more readily on big-ticket items with credit cards.

Receive payment faster than with checks. Funds are usually available within two business days of purchase.

Provide faster checkout. Your customers will enjoy rapid authorization and a choice of payment options.

Lower the risk of theft. There is less pilferage when you have less cash on hand.

Reduce problems with checks. Reduce the number of bad checks, returned checks, misreads, deposit paperwork, and more.

What is in it for the credit card company? A small payment from the store for every credit card purchase. Finance charges that the cardholder pays every month when he does not pay off his account balance. Depending on the card, another payment once a year from the cardholder just for the privilege of having the card, even if he does not buy anything with it.

Perhaps there is nothing intrinsically wrong with this system. Like other forms of credit, the thing in itself is not a snare. The question is, Where will it take you?

Leon had a credit card. He knew, of course, that the balance should be paid off every month. So when he or his wife made a purchase on credit, they usually deducted the figure from their checkbook balance to make sure they would not be taken by surprise when the bill came.

Eventually Leon changed credit card companies. Naturally,

he expected his last payment to his old company to wipe out the final balance. Naturally, he was perturbed when it did not. Over a thousand dollars remained to be paid!

Leon went back over his credit card statements. The light began to dawn. Even though he had paid for all his expenditures, he had sometimes paid late. The company had charged interest and late fees. When the statement came, Leon had looked at the interest figure and thought, "Uh-oh, I must have paid late. Do better next time." *But he had not always paid off the interest, and it continued to accumulate.*

Somehow the fact that his payments never wiped out the previous month's balance had not bothered him much. He had usually attributed it to the fact that his last payment must have arrived a little late. Do better next time!

When the truth became clear, he told his wife the story and said, "Obviously your husband has not learned to manage credit cards. I've put my credit card back in the desk drawer, and I'll use a debit card for the next while. I'm not telling you what to do, but every time you use a credit card, you risk losing more than you gain. Sorry about the air miles we won't earn. We could have bought three or four airline tickets with the money I already lost."

Leon was exceptionally foolish—or was he? One reads horror stories about people who hold a number of credit cards and run them to the limit with no clear idea of how they will ever pay them back. One observer remarked, "Borrowing has gone from a shameful vice to the national pastime. Instant gratification is our society's modus operandi. The consumer-debt rate is alarming. These trends can't continue forever."[9]

We gather from this that by running carelessly into debt, an individual not only harms himself but also casts a vote against the well-being of his country.

Sensible people agree—pay off your credit card each month, and do not buy more in any given month than you can pay for. One way to keep yourself from getting in trouble

> "A Federal Reserve survey found that 2003 was the year when, for the first time in history, Americans used their credit cards, debit cards, and other electronic payments more than checks."
>
> —Credit card newsletter

with credit cards is to deduct credit purchases in the checkbook as you incur them, just as if they were checks. If by some misfortune or miscalculation, you find yourself owing more on your credit card than you can pay off, borrow the money from the bank and pay off the credit card. You can pay the bank's lower rate of interest more easily than the credit card's high rate.

> *"If you use credit cards, you'll spend approximately 34 percent more money than if you use cash—and this assumes that you pay off your credit card bills every month. This figure comes straight from the credit card companies themselves."*[10]

Even sensible people often pay more for their credit cards than they realize. Did you notice this in the list of five reasons why business owners should accept credit cards? It is the number one item—to get their customers to buy more. Customers ask fewer questions and compare prices less when they know that all they have to do at the front counter is to say, "Charge." Even if they pay off their balance every month, using a credit card will hurt them if they buy more with their card than they would have bought without it.

Many people have given up trying to control their credit cards and have thrown them away. One man stopped just short of doing this. He cut away the top part of his card in order to get rid of the magnetic strip on the back side. He kept the rest of the card so that he would have the card number in case of an emergency. But he seldom used it, knowing it would feel pretty strange to hand cashiers a card they could not swipe. Of course, the reason he mutilated his card in the first place was to encourage himself to keep it out of sight.

He had twenty-nine credit cards, all of them maxed out. The deacon of his church, with his permission, took away all his cards but one. The deacon began calling credit card companies to explain that their customer wanted to pay off his debts. One credit card representative was not pleased. "That man pays his interest every month," he objected. "He is one of our best customers!"

If you find yourself in a long-term hole and see no end in sight, try calling the credit card company. Ask them to suspend the interest while you pay off the principal. You have already paid enough interest over the years that they should be happy with what they have already gotten from you. A number of people have gotten out of credit card bondage in this way.

Are debit cards (also known as bank cards) any less dangerous?

Well, at least they do not let you run yourself into a hole. A debit card works like both a check and a credit card, except that in this case the merchant makes immediate electronic contact with your bank. If you have enough in your checking account to cover the sale, you may buy. Otherwise, no.

With a credit card, you *should* keep track of your expenses. With a debit card, you are forced to do so. It is the only way to avoid bad moments at the checkout trying to buy items with money you do not have. "Buy now, pay later" does not work with debit cards. (Some dishonest people have found ways to abuse debit cards, but that does not apply to you.)

A record of your debit card transactions comes with your bank statement. In this respect it is again like both a check and a credit card. Since a debit card is less easily abused than a credit card, it is safer for most people.

In summary, you have a choice. You can wait to own a thing until you have the money for it, or you can buy it now. If you wait, you can enjoy what is known as "deferred gratification." If you cannot wait, enjoy your acquisitions. But remember, "Easy payments can make life hard."

"Buy on our installment plan!
100% down and <u>no</u>
monthly payments."

Managing a Large Debt

While you are in debt, keep no secrets. A banker naturally wants to know if you are borrowing from any other financial institution. (He does not necessarily care what your cousin hands you under the table.) Any creditor who wants to know all the sources of your income should in fact know, so he can judge what kind of risk he is looking at.

If the lender asks what you want the money for, tell him. The borrower is servant to the lender, even if the two are brethren. The lender might set the interest rate higher if you borrow to invest in a moneymaking enterprise than if you borrow to buy a house.

What if you get into a jam and cannot make a payment in time?

Speak frankly to your creditor. (A letter to a bank in such a situation is called a "cry letter.") Explain why you cannot pay. Ask for time. Tell the creditor when you think you can start paying again. Of course, be sure your lifestyle fits your situation. Living luxuriously does not make you very believable.

Most creditors, including bankers, are reasonably gracious with debtors who get into difficulties. Many of them are quite human and take a natural interest in people like you. They will not rush out to hold a sheriff's sale. Neither are most creditors eager to turn their debts over to collection agencies, if for no better reason than that the agencies take a percentage out of what they collect.

If you owe money to a Christian brother, do not relax too much. It is easy to forget that the borrower is servant to the lender and stretch the time too long. "And they that have believing masters, let them not despise them, because they are brethren; but rather do them service, because they are faithful and beloved, partakers of the benefit" (1 Timothy 6:2).

"Owe no man any thing, but to love one another" (Romans 13:8) is sometimes understood to mean you should never incur a debt. At the very least, it means you should make your payments on time!

Frankly, being slow to pay is not much different from robbing, no matter who the recipient is. "Thou shalt not defraud thy neighbour, neither rob him: the wages of him that is hired shall not abide with thee all night until the morning" (Leviticus 19:13). Defrauding, robbing, and procrastinating all fall into the same category. "I'd rather owe you than cheat you!" says the debtor to his creditor. That's nice. But if you owe someone overly long, what have you done but cheat him?

While you are in debt, should you feel less free than others to travel or replace your carpet? It might depend on the kind of debt. If you are paying for a farm in comfortable, regular installments, you probably have more liberty. If you are paying off a hospital bill—and scraping to do it—you might look irresponsible if you buy things you could do without for the time being. If the church is scraping to help you pay your bill, this is all the more true.

Should you give to the Lord when you have debts? Of course. We owe the Lord more than we owe anyone else. If you wait to give until you are out of debt, you might never give a penny.

Useful Terms

Bankruptcy. *Broke* and *bankrupt* are not the same thing. You go broke when you are out of ready cash or, at worst, out of all your assets. Someone goes bankrupt when he officially declares himself so deep in debt that it is impossible for him to repay his creditors.

There are different forms of bankruptcy, according to the U.S. Bankruptcy Code. Chapter 7 bankruptcy deals with a person who simply has nothing to pay. Chapter 11 bankruptcy deals with businesses that might be able to pay their debts but need a legal extension of time. Chapter 13 is for individuals who agree to pay out of their future income.

Once a person has gone bankrupt, he is legally no longer obligated to pay his debts, at least not by the dates originally agreed upon. In fact, if his creditors keep hounding him, he can threaten them with legal action unless they quit. Even before the point of bankruptcy, he can in certain cases send them a letter with a message such as the following:

> You are hereby notified under provisions of Public Law 95-109, Section 805-C, THE FAIR DEBT COLLECTION PRACTICES ACT, to CEASE AND DESIST in any and all attempts to collect the above debt.
> Your failure to do so WILL result in charges being filed against you with the state and federal regulatory agencies empowered with enforcement.[11]

In the past, bankruptcy was considered a personal disgrace and tragedy. Today many bankrupt persons are rather matter-of-fact about their condition. A friend who used to work for a small business remembers his irritation when a delinquent customer would take the attitude, "You can't touch me! I've gone bankrupt." Some would say, "If you don't stop sending us statements, we'll contact our lawyer." A number of customers wanted to start over with a new account, but that was where the business said no—not until they had paid their old debt.

Filing Chapter 11 or Chapter 13 bankruptcy keeps creditors away from one's door for a year. During that time, a court-appointed trustee helps the debtor manage his business. However, many have chosen not to go the bankruptcy route. One of the most famous examples is Harry Truman, whose clothing store failed when he was in his thirties. He refused to declare bankruptcy, and by working hard he eventually managed to pay off his debts.

For obvious reasons, people who never go into debt in the first place seldom go bankrupt. But since many of our brethren do not altogether shun debt, especially for business purposes, the question remains: Can a person find himself forced into bankruptcy through no fault of his own? As a rule, no. But one hears of reputable companies that have been brought to their knees by crushing lawsuits. No doubt it can happen.

We could raise all kinds of theoretical questions. However, we must remember that we have a Father who watches over all, and He directs the events in our lives more than we realize. We must take proper precautions in our business practices and trust God to honor that.

"Agree with thine adversary quickly," Jesus said in Matthew 5:25. It is not a matter of just being peaceable but being honorable. Honest, to put it bluntly. If you have incurred debts, you need to pay them.

Collateral. A young man bought a repossessed car from a bank. His father said to the banker, "Considering the age of the car, one would think it should be all paid off by this time. Isn't this unusual?"

The banker replied, "Sometimes a car is used for collateral." For example, a man borrows money to drill a well. Since the bank cannot take possession of a well, the man uses his car for collateral. If he cannot pay, the bank sells the car to recover the money.

The use of collateral is like the Bible practice of taking a pledge. In that case, the debtor handed over the collateral item until the debt was paid, as people often do at pawnshops. Regulations in Deuteronomy 24 forbade a creditor to take a millstone or a widow's cloak for a pledge. If he took a man's cloak, he had to return it before the sun went down.

In the case of a mortgage, the borrower pledges his real estate as a guarantee of payment.

The borrower needs to use common sense in relation to collateral. What about the young farmer who borrows to buy cows and then uses the cows as collateral for another loan to buy equipment? That is both foolish and dishonest.

Cosigning. We read in Proverbs 11:15 and other Scriptures that becoming surety for a stranger is foolish. In modern terms, if someone you do not know well asks you to cosign for a loan, you should say no. The other man may default, and then you will be stuck with the debt. "If thou hast nothing to pay, why should he take away thy bed from under thee?" (Proverbs 22:27). Good question!

It is wise to avoid cosigning even for a friend (Proverbs 6:1–5). But if the other person is someone you trust implicitly, and if you have enough assets to take on the payments for the loan if he dies, that *might* be a different matter.

Objections to Going Into Debt

These days, debt is supposed to be good for you. It improves your credit rating. People are encouraged to borrow money for this very purpose—so they can pay it back promptly and prove they are creditworthy. But some people refuse to go into any kind of debt, and their reasons are worth considering.

Debt presumes on an unknown, uncertain future. Remember the words of James 4:14: "Ye know not what shall be on the morrow."

Debt cuts down one's freedom, perhaps even the freedom to take care of his family, because paying off the debt comes first.

Debt may deny God an opportunity to work. God likes to do things in His own way, and Christians who step ahead of Him might miss something good that He had planned for them.

George Müller deserves his share of the page. As director of an orphanage established from scratch on donations, he determined never to buy anything unless he could pay for it at once—even food and medicine. Here is an excerpt from his diary.

December 1, 1842. For the last several months, money and supplies have continued to flow in without interruption as they were needed. There was no excess or lack. But nothing came in today except five shillings for needlework. We had only enough to supply our absolute need—milk. We were unable to purchase the usual quantity of bread.

Someone may ask, "Why don't you buy the bread on credit? What does it matter whether you pay immediately for it or at the end of the month? Since the Orphan Houses are the work of the Lord, can't you trust Him to supply you with money to pay the bills from the butcher, baker, and grocer? After all, the things you purchase are needed so that the work may continue."

My reply is this: If this work is the work of God, then He is surely able and willing to provide for it. He will not necessarily provide at the time we think that there is a need. But when there is real need, He will not fail us. We may and should trust in the Lord to supply us with what we require at present, so that there may be no reason to go into debt.

I could buy a considerable amount of goods on credit, but the next time we were in need, I would turn to further credit instead of turning to the Lord. Faith, which is maintained and strengthened by *exercise*, would become weaker and weaker. At last, I would probably find myself deeply in debt with no prospect of getting out of it.

Faith rests on the written Word of God, but there is no promise that He will pay our debts. The Word says, "Owe no man any thing" (Romans 13:8). The promise is given to His children, "I will never leave thee, nor forsake thee" (Hebrews 13:5). "He that believeth on him shall not be confounded" (1 Peter 2:6). We have no Scriptural grounds to go into debt.[12]

It is not clear to all Christians that they should follow this exact formula. Still, a surprising number of Christians come surprisingly close. And practically all of us go through moments when we are destitute of money or strength or other resources, and we find ourselves living like Müller whether we intended to do so or not. All other help fails, and we have to look straight up.

> *The only way to walk on water is one step at a time.*

We should also understand that Müller's policy involved much more than just the rule, "Never ask for money and never go into debt." His whole manner of living entered the picture—his sacrifices, his prayer life, his relationship with the Lord, and his absolute trust, even when he had to steer his whole enterprise within inches of disaster.

6. Giving

In this chapter, we will assume that you already give because you love the Lord. Here are some guidelines and ideas that hopefully you will find interesting and thought-provoking.

Simple Giving

"Sold!" The auctioneer's gavel crashes.

Amid laughter, a young man steps down from the platform. A bright-eyed young woman takes his place, and the auctioneer glances over her appraisingly. "Here's a fine-looking gal; you'll get a lot of work out of her. Let's start off at a hundred dollars a day, a hundred, a hundred, a hundred, two hundred, two hundred . . ."

"What's going on here?" a newcomer softly asks someone in the crowd.

"Oh, it's a slave sale. Not really, of course. We're raising money to build a new gymnasium for the Brookside Christian School. This is kind of a fun way to raise the money. We have an auction, and people offer themselves for sale. Whoever buys them has them for a day, or maybe a couple of days, and they work for the one who bought them. Of course, the buyer doesn't get his money's worth. But that's not the point. It's to raise money for the gymnasium."

"Looks like you're raising it pretty fast."

"Absolutely. And like I say, it's fun."

"Do you ever sell anything besides slaves to raise money?"

"Oh, sure. Last week we were selling quilts. It's amazing what some people will pay for a pretty one—far beyond what it's worth. That's because the money goes for relief or whatever. In fact, sometimes the same quilt gets sold two or three times."

"Two or three times?"

"Right, someone will buy a quilt and then say, 'Sell it again!' He never gets the quilt for himself. All he wants to do is contribute money. It sure adds up faster than bake sales and car washes. But we sometimes have them too. There are all kinds of painless ways to get people to give money."

In a tiny Sunday school room in a church basement, a small boy fingers a nickel. The young lady who is the teacher says, "Now let's all sing our offering song. I know most of you have nickels and dimes and quarters, but we'll sing about pennies because that's the way the song goes."

The class sings, " 'Dropping, dropping, dropping, dropping, / Hear the pennies fall; / Every one for Jesus! / He will get them all.' " The children hand around a tattered envelope and drop their coins into it.

"Yes, James?"

"How will Jesus get my nickel?"

"Hmm! Well, first it will go to the church secretaries, and they will count it along with the other money that people are giving. Then all the money will go the deacon, and he will send it to our mission in Costa Rica. The money will help to build a school for the boys and girls who live near the mission. Jesus said that when we do something kind for people, it's the same as doing it for Him. Do you think you understand?"

James smiles. Dropping that nickel had been a hard decision for him that morning. Usually his parents gave him a nickel on the way to church. However, his grandparents had brought him to church today, and no one had thought of giving James a nickel. But he did have a nickel of his own that a big boy had given him a few days before. James had been wondering how best to spend his nickel when suddenly the offering envelope was passed and he realized it was this nickel or none.

Which scene do you like better?

Rather, which one does the Lord like better? What would He say if He dropped in on the slave sale? If He thought it worth commenting on—after all, it was done in the name of Christianity— He would probably repeat His own words. "Take heed that ye do not your alms before men, to be seen of them: otherwise ye have no reward of your Father which is in heaven. . . . But when thou doest alms, let not thy left hand know what thy right hand doeth: that thine alms may be in secret: and thy Father which seeth in secret himself shall reward thee openly" (Matthew 6:1–4).*

Discreet giving shows up in various ways, large and small. Offering envelopes land in the offering basket blank side up. Hundred-dollar bills show up in the offering folded inside one-dollar bills. A needy church member learns that he is getting a replacement car because "some brethren" are getting together to help him buy it. Someone's rent for the month is paid by an anonymous friend.

How should you give discreetly to a friend in need if no church offering is taken for him at the time? Rather than giving directly to the person, you could give your gift to the deacon to pass on to him. This way the church gets the credit while you stay in the background.

What about the argument that a personal gift is more meaningful precisely because the receiver *does* know who it came from? Think of it this way: a gift of a cherry pie is the kind of thing you would give personally, and a gift of $800 is the kind of thing you would give by way of the church.

The apostle Paul summed it up in Romans 12:8. "He that giveth, let him do it with simplicity."

Giving With the Right Touch

Hardly any gift is more comforting than cold money when what you need is money! But admit it, money is rather cold by its very nature. Sometimes the things bought with money are cold too.

Why give our neighbors store buns if we have time to make buns of our own? Maybe we could give a dozen ears of sweet corn out of our own patch, or a handful of gladioluses from our garden. Or for friends who live farther away, give a song over the

---

* Other elements of carnality could enter the picture. Buying a pretty quilt is one thing; "buying" a pretty girl is another.

telephone. Even in these modern times, regular mail still works, and a handwritten note is far from being out of style.

Take time off from your job and help replace a friend's roof. Lend your tractor to someone, free of charge. Send your daughter to help a sister who has back trouble. Knit a pair of foot warmers for someone.

> *"I recall one widower mentioning that for years he and his family were the grateful recipients of covered dishes and other goodies, but seldom did anyone stay to eat the food with him."[1]*

When we give to people, we are giving to the Lord, and He likes the personal touch just as people do. After all, if God really needed our money, He could make it. If He needed the things money can buy, He could produce them too. "If I were hungry, I would not tell thee: for the world is mine, and the fulness thereof" (Psalm 50:12). What He really wants is our devotion. That is something He cannot make.

The early Christians in Macedonia understood this. Paul said of their generosity, "And this they did, not as we hoped, but first gave their own selves to the Lord" (2 Corinthians 8:5).

In simple words, do not just give money or things. Give *yourself*.

Give self-forgetfully. "What's in it for me?" people ask sometimes. Why, nothing. It is not for you at all. It is for someone in need.

Christmas baskets make the giver feel good, and there is nothing wrong with feeling good. But there is an appallingly long stretch between one Christmas and the next. What happens during the 364 days between the time you trip lightly down

> *"Though I bestow all my goods to feed the poor, and though I give my body to be burned, and have not charity, it profiteth me nothing."*
> *1 Corinthians 13:3*

Mr. Jones's walk and the time you return with another basket? What about the loneliness, perhaps, or the need for a pastime, or the need for transportation to the doctor? What about the lawn that needs to be mowed?

Meeting these needs is not as glamorous as giving pretty Christmas baskets. It involves patience, sweat, and some fumbling as the giver finds his way. But it separates the people who give self-forgetfully from the people who give occasional tokens for the good feeling they get out of it.

"I will have mercy, and not sacrifice," said the Lord in Matthew 9:13. Have mercy on people just because they need it, not because you hope your sacrifices will earn points for you in heaven.

Give respectfully. "Earn all you can; save all you can; give all you can." That is good advice, but there is one catch. Twisting all you can out of a man so you can give it to someone else (or even bestow it back on the man himself) does not follow Christian ethics. Often the most generous thing you can do for someone is to give him a good business deal.

Of course, this is a rather unexciting way to be generous. Face it, outright giving has a certain thrill. You are above the other person. You are handing something down to him. Even the Bible says, "The less is blessed of the better" (Hebrews 7:7). We wonder why people sometimes resent having to receive things from others, when it really should not be too surprising. In our own hearts, we can find the same sentiment in reverse—we can feel a little too good about our giving. We can feel powerful and superior.

Outright giving is a fact of life and a good one. But it is also a dangerous one, especially to the giver. To help prevent the danger to our souls, we can sometimes choose to give in a way that does not look like giving at all. Hiring a man and paying him a bountiful wage would be one way.

Someone did a favor for friends, and the friends wanted to pay. When the man who did the favor saw the size of their payment, he said, "That's not pay; it's a gift!" Still, because it was ostensibly a payment, it did not make him feel cheap. In some cases, however, payment would spoil the flavor of the favor.

In Old Testament times, the poor could glean in the fields after the reapers. This helped to preserve their self-respect while helping them to practice good work habits, which was their best way out of poverty. According to an old Hebrew story, a poor woman who gleaned in the field of a rich neighbor quickly caught his attention. He welcomed her into the circle of workers at lunchtime and made sure she had more than enough to eat. Quietly he told his reapers to let some handfuls fall on purpose for her. In the end, not surprisingly, he married her.

Most often in daily life, we show consideration to other people not by giving them an extra good deal but just by giving them a square deal. "There is greater love in justice than in pity."[2]

Give others the pleasure of giving. The story is astonishing. The prophet Elijah came upon a widow gathering two sticks to make a tiny fire under a tiny last meal before she and her son starved to death. What did he say? "Make me a little cake first!"

We usually think of Elijah's request as a test of the widow's faith. It was, but perhaps it was more. Maybe it actually made her feel good to give something to the man of God. As week followed week, she must have developed a real satisfaction to think that not only was Elijah helping her, but she was helping him. It was her barrel of meal, her cruse of oil, and her baking that sustained him. It was in her loft that the man of God resided, under her roof.

Yes, "it is more blessed to give than to receive," but sometimes the best donation is giving others the liberty to give.

Asking for money is a highly sensitive matter and not the kind of thing you do to warm up a friendship. But asking for a favor can be quite different. Here is one example: "Mr. Mifflin, something's flooding my laundry. I don't know what it is, and my husband's gone! Can you help me turn it off?" Here is another: "Mrs. Schubert, I just adore that shade of lilac. Do you think I could take a few slips from your bush and make starts of my own?"

> *Letting others give is not only good for them, it is good for us. A gift handed to us tends to keep us humble, since we are not in control of the gift.*

Missionaries have learned that it does not work well to build a church on foreign soil solely with North American funds. It is better to ask the local brothers and sisters for their contributions, however small they may be, because then they will have a church they can truly call their own. Could it be that members sometimes leave our churches, not because we failed to give them enough but because we failed to let them give enough?

Systematic Giving

"Three times in a year shall all thy males appear before the LORD thy God . . . and they shall not appear before the LORD empty: every man shall give as he is able" (Deuteronomy 16:16, 17). Systematic giving? Absolutely. Of course, the Israelites gave to the Lord at other times too. It was a flexible system, but it was a system.

"Upon the first day of the week let every one of you lay by him in store, as God hath prospered him, that there be no gatherings when I come" (1 Corinthians 16:2). Again, flexible but systematic giving.

Frances Havergal, author of the hymn "Take My Life, and Let It Be Consecrated, Lord, to Thee," wrote the following remarks. They are thought-provoking, though we may prefer to use "the Lord's Day" for what she called "the Sabbath."

"There is always a danger that just because we say 'all,' we may practically fall shorter than if we had only said 'some,' but said it very definitely. God recognizes this and provides against it in many departments. For instance, though our time is to be 'all' for Him, yet He solemnly sets apart the one day in seven which is to be specially for Him. Those who think they know better than God, and profess that every day is a Sabbath, little know what flood-gates of temptation they are opening by being so very wise above what is written. God knows best, and that should be quite enough for every loyal heart. So, as to money, though we place it all at our Lord's disposal, and rejoice to spend it all for Him directly or indirectly, yet I am quite certain it is a great help and safeguard, and, what is more, a matter of simple obedience to the spirit of His commands, to set aside a definite and regular proportion of our income or receipts for His direct service."[3]

On what basis should you give—gross income or net income? It should go without saying that if a businessman puts into the offering plate a tenth of all the money that passes through his hands, he will not be in business very long. If he sells a hammer for ten dollars retail and puts a dollar of that into the offering, he might have less than nothing left once he subtracts six dollars for the wholesale cost of the hammer, not to mention his other expenses.

Still, paying a tenth on his personal income makes sense,

and that before his personal income tax takes its bite. If someone waits to give until after he has paid off certain expenses, the game will never end, and he will always think of more expenses to get out of the way before he gives.

One way to teach children about giving is to hand them a coin on the way to church. They then put it in the offering. As they get older, a better way might be to give children a little money of their own out of which to give systematically. Help them figure how much it should be.

Give freely. It is possible to get too solemn about this matter of giving. For instance, we can argue for a long time about whether tithing is a Bible doctrine or a legalistic concept. Actually, the New Testament does not emphasize tithing as such. The nearest it comes to that might be Christ's words in which He rebuked the Pharisees for tithing but neglecting weightier matters, like judgment, mercy, and faith. He added, "These [more important matters] ought ye to have done, and not to leave the other [tithing] undone" (Matthew 23:23).

The Old Testament certainly taught tithing, and more. In fact, someone calculated that once the typical Israelite had given all his tithes and offerings, he had given about forty percent of his gains. But even in the Old Testament, freewill offerings were common. This foreshadowed New Testament times, when God wants us to be grown-up enough in our relationship with Him that we do not simply follow rules.

Still, "whatsoever things were written aforetime were written for our learning" (Romans 15:4), and New Testament Christians often take Old Testament hints on how things should normally be done.

Some of us by temperament like to have things spelled out. If God prefers to receive a certain fraction of our income in New Testament times, why does He not say so? Because He wants to treat us like adults. Must a husband order his wife to make breakfast? No, that would spoil their relationship. If he ordered every gift he got from her, that would do the same.

Why else has God not specified a tenth in our times? Maybe because a strict tithe would let well-to-do people off the hook. They could give 10 percent and still live like kings on the rest. And

"But if our Lord wanted us to do as she did [the widow who gave two mites], why did He not leave a clear command? How gladly then we would do it. Ah! there you have it. You want a command to make you do it. That would be just the spirit of the world in the church looking at *what* we give, at our giving all. And that is just what Christ does not wish and will not have. He wants the generous love that gives unbidden. He wants every gift to be a gift warm and bright with love, a true free-will offering."[4]

maybe because the needs around us are sometimes too immediate and overwhelming to even think of tithing. John the Baptist said, "He that hath two coats, let him impart to him that hath none" (Luke 3:11). That does not sound like a tithe.

Finally, God might be silent about tithing in our times because some people, at least at certain times in their lives, simply cannot afford that much. I do not know. All I can say is that people who give a tenth or more seem to be happy about giving it.

Give as you go along. Waiting till the end of the year to calculate whether or not you put enough into the offering will probably have only one result: you did not put in nearly enough, and you owe the Lord a thousand dollars! Better do your calculating as you go along.

You might be tempted to postpone your giving to the Lord so you can invest it in your business and make a greater profit. That way the Lord will supposedly end up getting even more next year. Not a good idea. One businessman, after thanking God for his prosperity, added, "And now that the new factory is finished, we'll really do some business. So instead of giving You Your share now, I'll put it all into expanding the business, and next year You will get a share to be proud of." About a year later, he found himself a hundred thousand dollars in debt. His comment: "God does not do business that way."[5]

If you wait until you have enough money to give, you will be waiting a long time. Studies of giving indicate that the rich do not give in proportion to their means. People with less money actually give a higher percentage of their income. One expert said, "Who does the giving in America? . . . The affluent are conspicuous only by their absence."[6]

An often-told story says that a young man, at a minister's

encouragement, once promised to give the Lord a tenth of all he earned. He had only ten dollars at the time, so he gave a dollar out of that to the Lord. Over the years, the Lord prospered him, and he became quite well-to-do. But a problem developed, so he asked the same minister to come for a visit. When the minister arrived at his beautiful home, the man said, "My income has increased to the point that the tenth I give to the Lord has become quite costly. Is there a way I can be let off my promise?"

"No, you should not go back on your promise," said the minister. "But there is one thing we can do. We can pray that the Lord will reduce your income so that you can afford to give a dollar again."

Judicious Giving

What if someone approaches you on the street and says, "Would you have a dollar for a cup of coffee?" See if you can take the fellow to a snack bar and buy a cup of coffee for him. Do not just give him a dollar, since the kind of person who asks for a dollar is probably broke for a reason. Perhaps he already drank up all the money he had (not in the form of coffee), and wants more for the same purpose.

Not every cause is equally worthwhile. A father and his boys stopped to pick up a hitchhiker. The hitchhiker told a sad story of how he had been robbed recently. Later one of the sons remarked to his father that he would have been glad to give the man some money to help make up his loss. But the father pointed out that they had not known the man or his circumstances. Where was he robbed? In a bar? It is better to give to people we know.

One man wrote:

> Even giving to worthy causes takes good judgment. A wealthy businessman observed, "Anyone can write a cheque. Anyone can give money away, but that is not the key to charity. To run a charitable organization carries a lot of responsibilities. It is 'to what project, to whom, how, how much, when, under what control, what follow-up, and how much should one give?' . . . Some people

have a simple idea. A good friend of mine said, 'I'm going to give everything to my church.' I said, 'You are going to kill that church. When there is money in excess in that church, the board of deacons for sure will say, "Let's build a daycare center. Let's build a home for the aged. Let's expand. Let's branch out. Let's help foreign missionaries. Let's help religious education. Let's do something in the medical field." But you cannot really do it all and do it well. The board will likely quarrel and might split the church.' "[7]

The question was once raised in a Sunday school: "If a brother has a need, should we automatically give? Or should we wait until we feel moved to give?" At this, a man from Austria spoke up in his distinctive way: "If someone has neets, he has neets! Moofed or not moofed."

Well said. There is the fact, though, that we should give intelligently. Too much help might be the wrong thing for a struggling brother. Maybe he must learn to sink or swim. Or maybe the church has already decided to help him in some other way.

The world is crying with needs, and Jesus said, "Give to every man that asketh of thee" (Luke 6:30). Yet Jesus Himself once walked into a virtual hospital and healed just one person (John 5:1–9). On another occasion when His disciples said, "All men seek for thee," He replied, "Let us go into the next towns, that I may preach there also: for therefore came I forth" (Mark 1:38).

Some recent mail illustrates the point. The plea begins like this:

Dear Friend,
    I don't know how anyone can turn away a hungry child . . .
    But it's happening!
    <u>Churches, food pantries and feeding centers across the country have run out of food.</u> Destitute families have nowhere else to turn. Mothers are terrified their babies will starve!
    And the children just keep suffering . . . they go to bed hungry and in pain.
    Desperate mothers are standing in line, hoping against hope that they will get a little food for their children. . . .

But, all too often, the food simply runs out. When it does, even the volunteers can't choke back the tears. . . .

Send $7 with the $7 Coupon, and you will personally ensure the delivery of 50 LBS. OF URGENTLY NEEDED FOOD TO HUNGRY GIRLS AND BOYS ACROSS OUR GREAT LAND!

This plea comes from *Feed the Children,* self-described as "a nonprofit, international, Christian relief organization which has distributed food and other assistance to needy children and their families in all 50 states, the District of Columbia, and 94 other countries since 1979." This description helps a little, but anyone wanting to contribute would do well to contact its people personally. Since it claims to operate in every state, one might not have to travel far to verify that these people actually hand out food to hungry children.

Save your best giving for the church. If someone knocks on your door wanting a contribution for a worthy local project, consider giving something as a goodwill gesture because he or she is a neighbor. Even then, sift out the requests. The other day I got a telephone call from someone who said, "We all like firefighters, don't we?" He was trying to get contributions to support a musical concert as a way of helping the firefighters. In a case like that, see if you can offer something that goes directly to the firefighters rather than the concert.

One organization specializes in giving dying children whatever they wish—a visit from a famous person, a trip to Disney World, or whatever. What should you tell solicitors when they call? You might explain your real beliefs—that you believe a dying child is about to get all his wishes at once and that you are already contributing to more urgent needs than this that have more wholesome solutions. Or you might simply say, "Is it all right if I decline for personal reasons?"

Going the polite route by hearing the solicitor out before you decline will probably not make him any happier. After declining in a roundabout fashion, one person got this rebuke: "In all honesty, sir, it would have been better if you had just said no at the beginning." One solicitor put it this way: "A yes is great; a no is good."

The same principle applies when you get various requests for money in the mail. Often the request is accompanied by some little gift, such as self-adhesive address labels. You feel guilty for using these things without paying for them, so your first impulse might be to send them enough at least to cover the cost of the stickers. Oops, once you do that, they will send you a thankful receipt, and sooner or later, more labels!

Perhaps the wisest thing to do, once you recognize the senders, is to discard their envelope without even opening it. If they are persistent, cross out your own address and write, "Refused. Return to sender." Back into the mailbox!* Some of those causes might be all right, but you cannot support them all. Let others support the mail-order causes; you support the church.

Balance local and distant giving. The more distant the need, the less we need to be concerned about it. But the more urgent the need, the more we need to be concerned about it, even if it is distant. The urgent supersedes the local.

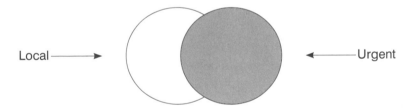

Thus we might decide against installing a new kitchen, which is a local need, in favor of helping starving children in some other country, which is a more urgent need. This does not mean we should never improve our kitchens just because there are always starving children somewhere. But it does mean we rightly allow other people's needs to supersede our own privileges. We can put off our wants for a while or do without them entirely.

"Charity begins at home" is an old saying, and a true one as far as it goes. "If any provide not for his own, and specially for

---

* Regrettably, not all mail can be returned.

those of his own house, he hath denied the faith, and is worse than an infidel" (1 Timothy 5:8). We have no business giving to some distant, exotic land if another need just as pressing is closer home. But we can go to the other extreme, minding only our own needs, the needs of our family and friends, and the needs of our congregation—thus failing to enrich people beyond our horizons and, in the process, failing to enrich ourselves. Yes, charity begins at home, but it does not stop there.

> *"The naked every day he clad*
> *When he put on his clothes."*

Before you decide where to give, put yourself in the other fellow's place. An American doctor who went to Africa wrote home something like this: "I feel bitter when millions are spent in America to make a great hospital better while at the same time my patients suffer from ghastly infections because there are holes in my surgical gloves."

We cannot do everything about everything. But we can do something about something. Walk down to the world's ocean of misery, and take out your bucketful.

Give just a bit recklessly. Let us not assume that we can wait to give until the person who asks for help deserves it. God "sendeth rain on the just and on the unjust." He can calculate how much people deserve, but since He deals with mortals, He knows that calculation is not enough. There must be compassion.

Robert lived not far from a gas station. Occasionally someone would drop in and ask for money to buy gas to get to Jonestown. Should he help?

Robert chose not to give the people cash. Rather, he would call ahead to the gas station and say, "A man is going to drop in at your station for gas. He's driving a green Chevy van. Give him twenty dollars' worth, and I'll pay you for it later today." Putting it on his charge account or credit card would have worked too.

Giving like this has its downside. Strangers would promise to reimburse Robert, at which he would smile inside. They never did. Robert's wife gave a meal to a stranger, but the children later found most of it tossed into a snowbank. Still, the giving was not merely to a stranger but to the Lord, who sees all and rewards all in His own way.

"In the morning sow thy seed, and in the evening withhold not thine hand: for thou knowest not whether shall prosper, either this or that, or whether they both shall be alike good" (Ecclesiastes 11:6).

Cheerful Giving

"God loveth a cheerful giver" (2 Corinthians 9:7). He also accepts from a grudger, so you need not wait to give until your attitude is just right. But you might as well enjoy giving because there is plenty to be cheerful about.

Giving strengthens us, as the following testimony makes clear.

"In stories of survivors of the Nazi death camps, an attitude of determined giving was one of the things that distinguished the survivors from those who perished. If a prisoner was on the verge of starvation, but he had a crust of bread or a scrap of a potato that he could share with his comrade in suffering, he was psychologically and spiritually capable of surviving.

"A survivor of Treblinka described it this way: 'In our group we shared everything, and the moment one of the group ate something without sharing it, we knew it was the beginning of the end for him.' "[8]

A housewife invited to her home for lunch a woman whose husband had left her. During their conversation, she discovered how little her friend had. But to her surprise, her friend pulled out two cards, delicately hand-painted, and said, "I made these for you."

"Oh," the hostess said, "you didn't need—"

"Yes, I did," the visitor interrupted quietly. "Giving is the way I keep going."[9]

Giving is good for nearsightedness. The more you put into your next life, the more you will value the next life and the less you will value your present life. If you invest too much in the present life, you might wonder in a crisis why you are so eager to save your present life. Giving reminds us that this life and

"God bestows His gifts with apparently unequal hand that our love may have the high privilege of restoring the equality. . . . Everything has been so ordered that love shall have room to work."[10]

the next are not all that far apart.

Giving improves the love among us. If someone has a loss, even if he can afford it, we expect him to accept at least some help from the brotherhood. It is good for him, and it is good for the rest of us.

Giving catches the attention of our Lord. It is interesting to note the puzzled reaction of the righteous at the final judgment when the Lord tells them He has noted their kind deeds: "When saw we thee an hungred, and fed thee? or thirsty, and gave thee drink? When saw we thee a stranger, and took thee in? or naked, and clothed thee?" (Matthew 25:37, 38). Evidently they had not stopped to feel good about what they had done. They had simply done it because it needed to be done. Giving is worthwhile even if we get no particular thrill out of it. The Lord sees it all.

Giving is a form of investment. "He that hath pity upon the poor lendeth unto the LORD; and that which he hath given will he pay him again" (Proverbs 19:17). However, the Bible does not emphasize this concept too much. It is buried in the middle of other bits of wisdom. Too easily we get the idea that if we put money into the offering, we will get money back. Actually, the Lord will give us much more than money—things that money cannot buy.

For example, what kind of rewards do you want in heaven? Money, no. I cannot think of a better reward than friends. Some of these will be friends we have helped heavenward with our investments in them—investments of money, time, and effort. They will be a special reward to us.

It is a pleasant pastime to watch people coming off airplanes at the airport and meeting their loved ones. We share in their pleasure. Would you not like to stand inside the gate of heaven and watch people coming in? Maybe sometime we will.

A farmer once confided to a writer that the money he gave to missions would have bought several farms. The writer remarked,

"He is a poor man, but he is an incredibly happy man."[11] No wonder.

"Cast thy bread upon the waters: for thou shalt find it after many days" (Ecclesiastes 11:1).

Brotherhood Assistance

All kinds of brotherhoods have their ways of helping each other. The Masons do. Firefighters do. Members of labor unions do. Not surprisingly, God's people do too.

The early Christian church "had all things common." It seemed perfectly natural. They had a new faith in common, and they were having a kind of honeymoon with it and with each other. But soon it became obvious that they were overlooking some needy people, so they set up a more regular system. Rather than dampening the love they had for each other, the deacon system helped to extend that love.

Obviously this was a religious arrangement, not a secular one. The church helped widows. The church helped the blind and crippled. The church helped people with leprosy. Deacons were central figures in the life of the early Christians.

Thus it remained for centuries. The church did much to relieve human misery both inside and outside the church. Much misery remained, but most people accepted this as a fact of life.

In more recent years, humanitarians understandably rebelled at the thought that widespread poverty is inevitable. However, they also looked away from the church and charitable organizations for their answer. Governments began doing what churches were not getting done. Governments did much to relieve human misery. Still much misery remained. In fact, some observers charged the welfare system with creating misery even as it relieved misery.

In the meantime, churches kept their charitable functions but lost their central position in the field of charity. People outside the churches looked more and more to the government for aid and less and less to the church.

In fact, as time went on, people within the church did the same. Deacons were no longer relief givers, for members were getting relief from government programs along with other secular institutions such as insurance. Deacons were basically assistant ministers with some vestigial duties like visiting the sick and perhaps handling church money.

All this was not lost on every observer. During a revival in one church, the brethren came forward with a statement on the subject. Here is the statement as it appeared sometime later in the "Rules and Discipline" of that church.

One of the questions that faces the church today is, How can we maintain a brotherhood attitude in an economic climate that is geared to make the individual feel self-sufficient? Individuals actually are becoming more and more dependent on financial establishments that are created to ease economic stress when adverse conditions arise. One of the results of such a trend is that we will eventually become subservient to a central government bureaucracy. This type of situation would certainly not be favorable to relaying our faith to the rising generations, but would eventually bring us to bow down to national leaders, thanking them for our daily bread rather than worshiping the true God.

The insurance companies of America dominate much of the wealth of this country, which in turn indicates the degree to which men trust in them. Where the purchase of insurances by church members has become the norm, there has been a slow but sure decline in one of the ordained offices of the Biblically organized church, namely, the deacon office.

Accompanying the spiritual awakening and revival at the forming of [our church], there was a renewed desire to restore the Bible practices to full force, including the Scriptural function of the deacon office.

According to the Scriptures (Acts 6:1–7 and I Timothy 3:8–12), God has made provision for all the needs of the brotherhood. . . .

In light of these truths, we feel it is very important that [our church] continue to rise to her God-appointed opportunity in promoting a true brotherhood in this materialistic age.

We do not favor an approach that is merely another insurance organization with some modifications. But rather we wish to follow the Bible way in caring for and sharing with an unfortunate member or one who is in need.

The following outline, we feel, is a practical approach to this issue:

1. There needs to be continued teaching on the evils and dangers of being involved in worldly organizations and what it does to us. (2 Corinthians 6:14–18)

2. We need to teach the importance of trusting in God rather than in the inventions of men. (Psalm 118:8)

3. We must maintain the assistance aspect of the deacon office as it was originally intended. (Acts 6:1–7)

4. The deacon shall be supplied with sufficient funds so he can exercise his office. These funds become available by lifting regular, realistic offerings. (1 Corinthians 16:1, 2)

5. All contributions to the deacon fund are to be strictly on a voluntary basis in order to bring a close degree of equality. (2 Corinthians 8:15)

6. A central treasury shall be avoided. All funds are to be kept by the local deacon of every congregation. (Titus 1:5)

7. When a need arises that is more than a local congregation can bear, the deacon, at the direction of the local bishop, shall ask for help from the deacons of the other congregations in his district. If the need is still not met by a district appeal, the deacon and bishop where the need exists shall then, upon the agreement of the bishops, call all the deacons of [our denomination] together and pool the resources to have the need filled. (Acts 11:29, 30; 2 Corinthians 9:5–7)

8. Local congregations and districts are encouraged to offer assistance to spiritual, conservative-minded congregations other than [ours] when appeals come for help and they are in a position to do so. (Galatians 6:10)

9. We look favorably toward members eliminating all insurances and following the Bible-approved way of life, which means not living to the full limits of our income so we may have something to save and to give. Also that we bear one another's burdens and suffer with the member who suffers. (1 Corinthians 12:26; 2 Corinthians 12:14; Galatians 6:2)

10. Every congregation shall decide on a maximum level that may be accumulated in the deacon fund so that we may avoid having people trust in a large established fund, but rather that they trust God and His people. (Psalm 37:25)

Can such a system work? Well, the original statement, adopted in 1970, said, "We believe that God is waiting to bless our church in a way that we have not experienced heretofore if we are willing to honor Him in this way." A revised and reaffirmed statement twenty-five years later simply said, "We believe that God will continue to bless our church as we are willing to honor Him in this way."

Can such a system be abused? Absolutely. One writer remarked, "We believe our present-day application of mutual aid is under extreme test. Easy credit has caused many to increase the size of their businesses or farming operations and has resulted in much bigger losses when calamity strikes, whether through fire, storm, or financial reverse. If the loss is considerable, congregations are left grappling with how to pay for it."[12]

Then too, it is easy for even well-meaning members to develop the attitude, "I'll use my own best judgment, and if I get into trouble, the church will bail me out." No; each member is responsible for his own finances. The church respects this and does not like to interfere. A person who is cast on his own resources learns lessons in hard work, thrift, management, values, and priorities. He learns to mind his own business—indeed he *has* to, keeping his nose to the grindstone. Further, he becomes "rich in faith" because he is depending on God rather than on a tangible organization.

A secular organization trying to operate like the church program described above would not work. But a church full of spiritual people can make it work, and the more spiritual they are, the more naturally it will work. If the shoe fits, wear it, and the shoe of brotherhood assistance fits godly people perfectly.

7. Thinking Out Loud

Cashless Society

Cold hard cash has won considerable respect for thousands of years. But within our lifetime, something has been rapidly changing. Credit cards, debit cards, and smart cards are here. The part of the card that looks the least interesting—the dark stripe on the back—holds a magnetic record of the information that makes the card work. A smart card carries a computer chip.

> *"No card, no cash. He should have checked first. A thief tried to hold up a branch of the Toronto Dominion bank in St. Catharine's. Despite his threats, no one gave him any money. In that particular branch, the only cash available was in the automatic teller machines!"*[1]

Cards are unquestionably convenient. They outdo counting change or writing out a check. These days you can fill up at the gas pump by swiping a card on the spot. You do not have to walk into the store or even sign your name.

But cards create unique problems. In the old days, if someone stole your wallet, he could spend only the money you had in the wallet. These days a thief who has your credit card can spend "your" money right up to your credit limit of perhaps thousands of dollars. Credit card companies are sympathetic to people whose cards are stolen, encouraging them to report missing cards as soon as possible and not requiring them to stand good for purchases they never made. But credit card theft and fraud accounts for millions of dollars lost each year. Debit cards can be misused as well.

One should not panic over each new and strange development. Some of us are old enough to remember the suspicion with which people regarded bar codes when they first appeared on store items. Some people even wondered if they should patronize stores using bar codes. With time and observation, nearly everyone decided the new system was as safe as it was convenient. Of course, bar codes helped to prepare people's minds for the next development.

Where can you keep your credit or debit card securely? In an inside coat pocket? In the lining of your hat? In your shoe? Shall you tie it to yourself with a string?

The modern solution seems to be to shrink the information found on a card, putting it on a microchip so tiny it can be implanted under your skin. You will never absent-mindedly walk away from a store counter without it, nor will anyone steal it. And what could be easier than to pass your chip-implanted hand over a scanner to register your purchase? Scanners already read the bar codes on grocery boxes.

This brings to mind the words of an ancient manuscript: "And he causeth all, both small and great, rich and poor, free and bond, to receive a mark in their right hand, or in their foreheads: and that no man might buy or sell, save he that had the mark, or the name of the beast, or the number of his name" (Revelation 13:16, 17). This sounds eerily like today's news. Not too long ago, people thought the mark described in this passage sounded like some kind of tattoo. Now they see a different kind of fulfillment.*

Many people—even ungodly people—know about the mark of the beast. On being asked if they would accept such a mark, they would probably say no. Yet if the day comes that they must choose between buying and not buying, or selling and not selling, what will they choose? Even many religious people will accept the mark. After all, they can explain away this Bible passage as easily as they do many other passages.

Here are some refreshing observations.

Some very unsound papers and books concentrate heavily on the end time and what to avoid, but they include very little on how to be ready spiritually for eternity. . . .

When we look at Revelation 13:16–14:1, where do we put the emphasis? Often it is placed on receiving a mark on the right hand or the forehead. Some people put much emphasis on not being able to buy or sell, even to the extent of advising what to invest in so as not to lose money. Others put the main

---

* In another few years, they might see another. It is right to be aware of certain modern developments without making rash pronouncements about them.

emphasis on having a number or on the number 666. Still others emphasize the nature of the mark of the beast.

From Revelation 7:3 and 13:8, it seems clear that it is important not just to avoid the mark or number of the beast, but to have the seal of the Father and to have our name written in the Lamb's Book of Life.[2]

We can have our names written in the Book of Life even now. That is reassuring, for it will help protect us from accepting the mark of the beast.

However, it will not necessarily protect us from the persecution or privation that might come from *not* having the mark. One Christian worried, "We are part of a system that has us wrapped in. What if the day comes that we can't buy or sell? Then what? We'll be walking the streets begging and sleeping in people's barns."

Perhaps this is what the Bible refers to by the words, "These are they which came out of great tribulation. . . . They shall hunger no more, neither thirst any more" (Revelation 7:14, 16). Tribulation, hunger, and thirst are real enough for other people; and we are ordinary people too. We cannot claim immunity from these problems.

But notice the other expressions: "came out . . . no more . . . any more." The Lord will have His own way of comforting us even in troubling times; and when these problems are past, we shall look forward to a glorious—cashless—future. "For the Lamb which is in the midst of the throne shall feed them, and shall lead them unto living fountains of waters: and God shall wipe away all tears from their eyes" (Revelation 7:17).

Living by Faith

Where do we draw the line between living by faith and providing for ourselves? How much should we wait on the Lord, and how much should we move ahead on our own? We do not want to doubt providence, but we do not want to be presumptuous either.

The Lord has not drawn exactly the same line for everyone.

Jesus praised a widow for giving her last two mites. He reassured the disciples that they had done the right thing when Peter said, "Behold, we have forsaken all, and followed thee" (Matthew 19:27). He sent out the disciples, telling them to take nothing for their journey: "No scrip, no bread, no money in their purse" (Mark 6:8). Of Himself He said, "The Son of man hath not where to lay his head" (Matthew 8:20).

Yet Jesus borrowed a boat, a donkey, and an upper room without uttering a word to suggest that the owners were wrong in having those things. He sharply criticized scribes and Pharisees for devouring widows' houses (Matthew 23:14), implying that widows ought to have something to live on. When He said, "Let him which is on the housetop not come down to take any thing out of his house" (Matthew 24:17), He meant that the time might come to flee from one's house; but He also implied that it was all right to own a house until that time. When He said, "I was a stranger, and ye took me in" (Matthew 25:35), He implied the same. "In" where? In under one's own roof, evidently.

Not only does the Lord draw different lines for different people, but He draws lines differently for different times in people's lives.

God led Israel through a wilderness forty years, supplying manna day by day. But the time came when God brought Israel into the Promised Land and said, in effect, "Now I am going to stop giving you the finished product. I will start giving you the raw materials and let you do it."

At the close of Jesus' ministry, He asked His disciples, "When I sent you without purse, and scrip, and shoes, lacked ye any thing? And they said, Nothing. Then said he unto them, But now, he that hath a purse, let him take it, and likewise his scrip: and he that hath no sword, let him sell his garment, and buy one" (Luke 22:35, 36). He was saying, "Things are going to be different

"Others may be allowed to succeed in making money, or may have a legacy left to them, but it is likely God will keep you poor because He wants you to have something far better than gold, namely, a helpless dependence upon Him, that He may have the privilege of supplying your needs day by day out of an unseen treasury."[3]

now. Physically, I will be gone. I will not necessarily provide for you in the future as I have provided in the past. There will be times when you must provide for yourselves."

> *We must have the proper attitude toward people who have more than we do (not jealous), and toward people who have less (not disdaining).*

The same principles apply today.

Some Christians live by faith day in and day out, often not knowing how God can possibly supply their present needs. The stories they tell are thrilling! But we need not feel guilty if God has not called us to a lifestyle like that. No doubt we will have moments in our lives when we also come to the end of our resources—whether financial, physical, or emotional—and God comes to the rescue. We may praise Him for these times without thinking we must have this kind of thing constantly.

He calls many people to go through life, or at least a part of it, wondering where their next dollar is coming from; and He supplies it in the nick of time. But He calls others to operate businesses and hold down jobs and contribute to His work in that way. There is as much to be learned about God from earning money and calculating

> *A young child owns little and needs to own little. All his needs are supplied!*

expenditures as from being unable to earn money and letting God supply all our needs.

Once we start trying to follow the patterns used by other people, we run into logical difficulties. Suppose we decide to walk penniless down the road in obedience to Jesus' command, "Take neither gold, nor silver, nor brass in your purses." What about His other commands in the same breath—for instance, "Go not to the Gentiles"? What about "Heal the sick, cleanse the lepers, raise the dead, cast out devils"? I am not saying it is wrong to be a penniless missionary if that is what God calls you to do. But it is wrong to feel obligated to do what Christ told His disciples to do on an isolated occasion during His earthly ministry.

While the Lord may bless people who live poorer than we, He might also bless people who do things that seem extravagant to us. Uncle Paul remarked, "When people find out we're

> *Passenger to pilot: "I put my trust in the Lord!"*
> *Pilot to passenger: "I do too, but I watch the gauges."*

going to Florida for the winter, they say, 'That must be expensive.' And I tell them, 'It's expensive to go to the hospital too!' And that's where we would go if we didn't go to Florida." Now do not rush off to Florida just because Uncle Paul said that. But do recognize that he had a point. We should not judge others too quickly.

We need to remember, too, that the Lord might draw the line differently for us at different stages in our journey. Uncle Paul had not spent every winter of his life in Florida. The apostle Paul put it this way: "I know both how to be abased, and I know how to abound: every where and in all things I am instructed both to be full and to be hungry, both to abound and to suffer need" (Philippians 4:12).

The Pinch of Poverty

You know you are poor when—

- An excited friend calls you about a great bargain in town, and you simply say "Thanks." For you cannot buy the item, cheap as it is, even though passing it up means you must pay twice as much later. You wonder what your friend thinks of you.
- A little money finally comes, and all the needs you have been putting off suddenly scream for your attention. The half-inch-deep laundry soapbox, the holes in your children's outgrown shoes, the unevenly worn tire, the medicine that has run out . . .
- A friend chuckles over "these folks who can't scrape even five dollars together," and you do not chuckle.
- You wonder why you ever started feeding the birds, and you wince inwardly every time the children pray for a dog.
- You put ten dollars' worth of gas into your tank so you can go and buy two quarts of milk to tide you over until the paycheck comes.
- You know fifty-seven uses for duct tape and wish you had some.
- You have to borrow the Vise-Grip from the kitchen faucet every time you need it.

- You keep retaping your child's glasses.
- Your spouse gives you a small bottle of glue for your birthday, explaining that it didn't cost much and you really do need the glue.
- You wonder how soon your family will be hitchhiking to church on Sunday morning.
- You cannot make it to your son's out-of-state wedding without a friend's help.
- You miss the family reunion because the money will not stretch far enough to take you there. (You wait to call until it is too late for someone to say, "Come anyhow; we'll help you out.")
- You read, "If thy brother be waxen poor" in Leviticus 25, and suddenly realize that you are that brother.
- You are down to one egg and wonder how to use it in a family-size recipe.
- You go to the mailbox, hoping some relief will come. It does not, and you think, "Now what, Lord?"
- You feel a certain kinship with the down-and-out.
- You wonder what it would be like to be *really* poor, and how much you really know about poverty after all.*

Painful as it is, poverty has advantages. For one thing, it makes you work harder. Most people move faster when they are being pinched.

Poverty brings the feeling of weakness; and as the apostle Paul said, "When I am weak, then am I strong" (2 Corinthians 12:10). Often it helps you realize that you cannot control your own situation, and that God wants to show that He is in control. You can be ever so desperate for money, but your desperation only underscores the fact that "it is he that giveth thee power to get wealth" (Deuteronomy 8:18).

Poverty is an eye opener. The sensations of it are different than you might expect. For instance, someone noticed the "exhaustion" of being poor, which a person who always has had money would probably never think of.

---

* Have you tried sleeping in a telephone booth recently? Some people have.

Poverty strengthens you in the struggle against sin. A person who has everything money can buy may have a hard time coming to a screeching halt when he is confronted by temptation. He has everything else—why can he not have sin too? In contrast, "he that hath suffered in the flesh hath ceased from sin" (1 Peter 4:1). Someone who is used to being denied even of permissible things will not have a serious struggle when he is denied of impermissible things.

Poverty puts you on the same level with Jesus Christ and other wonderful people. You can relate to poor folks comfortably. Having been poor, you realize that the worst thing you can do with any money you do have is to spend it on things that supposedly put you on a higher social level than people around you.

Poverty makes you sensitive to the physical and spiritual needs of others. When you are full, you think less about people who do not have enough. Hunger for natural food does not seem real. Spiritual hunger does not seem real either. This creates an impediment on both sides of mission work. If people are too hungry for food, they are not open to the Gospel; and if people who have the Gospel are too full, they are not inclined to spread the Gospel anyway.

Should you therefore pray that God would make you poor? Not anymore than you should pray for persecution, despite its advantages. "Give me neither poverty nor riches," says Proverbs 30:8, and the context points out that both rich and poor have their own temptations. Ideally, one should be neither filthy rich nor dirt-poor.

Do not pray for poverty, but do not panic if it comes. Be especially careful when discussing it in front of your children. Doubtless, too many parents have given their children the impression that living by faith while squeezing a budget is a horrid assignment. Too often they spill out their doubts and worries instead of taking the view, "Let's work hard together, sacrifice where we can, and see what the Lord will do for us."

One man remembers from his boyhood that his father would go away on church business and receive some money for his services. But before he returned home, he would find some family poorer than his own and would give them his money, saving just enough to get home. Once home, he had to face his wife's question, "Did you bring any money?" "That's what I want to talk to you about," he would say with a grin. Soon they would gather the children around them, explain that they had no money, and pray that the Lord would supply their needs. He always did.

Finally, if poverty comes in large or small measure, remember to count your advantages. Poverty brings not only pinch but also pleasure. The rich man's wife will never know the joy a poor man's wife gets from owning a new, full, sweet-smelling box of laundry soap.

The World's Have-nots

There is poverty, and then there is *poverty*. You can be below the official poverty line and still sing, "There's a roof up above me, I've a good place to sleep, / There's food on my table and shoes on my feet." Some people—appallingly many people, in fact—have none of these things. Millions suffer from malnourishment, exposure, and disease, especially in parts of Asia, Africa, and Latin America.

This, of course, is an old fact. Because we have often heard it before, and because we figure we cannot do much about it anyway, most of us have developed a certain numbness about the subject. Even Jesus sounded resigned when He remarked, "Ye have the poor with you always" (Mark 14:7). Many poor people of His time were not just idyllically poor; they were literally hungry, with little relief in sight.

> *"I am only one, but I am one. I cannot do everything, but I can do something. And because I cannot do everything, I will not refuse to do what I can do."*[4]

But there is another side to the subject. Jesus went on to say, "And whensoever ye will ye may do them good." Although He did not eliminate hardship on earth, He said and did enough to show that He cared about the problem.

And how may we "do them good"?

Given a few minutes to think, many people would come up with one or more of the following answers. (1) Try to influence politicians and economists to create better conditions for the have-nots. (2) Conserve world resources so there is more for everyone. (3) Reach out directly to the have-nots, helping them and teaching them to help themselves. We will think about each of these in the paragraphs that follow.

Option 1 is called political activism. No doubt political activists have influenced the "powers that be" to be more generous and fair in their dealings with poor countries. And certainly no rich nation has been too generous or too fair.

The United States, for example, has over the years contributed billions in loans and grants to less developed countries. It has given favorable trading terms to most nations. So the record of the United States on this point is not entirely bad.

But some people assume that the wealth of rich nations in itself proves their guilt. The idea seems to be, "If you're rich and I'm poor, you must have stolen from me somehow." That is much too simplistic.

Still, when you compare the vast resources of the United States with what it actually contributes to the needs of poor nations, the charitable percentage is quite small. And it has become smaller in recent years. During the Cold War, the United States and Russia competed against each other for the friendship of poor countries. When the Cold War ended, that motivation ended.

Here is where politics comes in. Many people assume political activism to be as important as not wasting food. One writer said, "Actually, the two realms—conserving resources at home and taking on economic and political issues—are as inseparable as the yolk and white of a scrambled egg."[5]

But Jesus separated the two. When offered political power, He refused it—once in the wilderness when the devil offered it, and once when people wanted to forcibly make Him a king. Political activism was conspicuously absent from what Jesus and the apostles did. Jesus said things like "Who made me a judge or a divider over you?" and "My kingdom is not of this world."

There was oppression and injustice aplenty in those days. But even when Jesus and the apostles were called before rulers and had a golden opportunity to give political advice, they stuck to giving their personal testimony and pointing out the spiritual need of their listeners. They knew that when spiritual issues are taken care of, other matters begin to take care of themselves.

John the Baptist came close to giving political advice when he told tax collectors, "Exact no more than that which is appointed you" and told soldiers, "Do violence to no man, neither accuse any falsely; and be content with your wages." But that is still a far cry from political activism.

Option 2 involves living frugally. Jesus approved of frugality, for after feeding the five thousand, He said, "Gather up the fragments that remain, that nothing be lost" (John 6:12). Living savingly is an art. (See Chapter 3 on economizing.)

But conserving resources does not in itself put more food into the hands of people who need it. Hungry people generally have no money to buy food, which is why they are hungry in the first place. We are called to do more than just "live simply" as our duty to the have-nots.

What is more, cutting down the number of things we buy might not help the poor of some other country. (Unfortunately, buying these things might not help them either, if the profits end up in the pockets of multinational corporations rather than in the hands of local workers.) The fact is, refusing to eat bananas because banana workers get paid too little, or refusing to buy a carpet because it was made by child labor in Pakistan, will probably not solve any problems.

Option 3 means going or sending someone personally to reach the have-nots. This is what Jesus did. He came to this planet and became poor. He touched the poor folks, and they touched Him. He "went about doing good." His actions complemented the Gospel He preached. This option has the most promise.

Conservative churches have rightly closed the door on political activism, but they have also opened so many doors in foreign

"In its growth and prosperity, America has sometimes used natural resources recklessly. Is it right for 5 percent of the world's population to use 20 percent of the world's resources? Where that use is due to extravagance and waste, it is wrong."[6]

"Too often the haves and have-nots are strikingly related to the dids and the did-nots."[7] But this is more likely to be true in a prosperous country than in a less developed and oppressed country.

countries that we have no right to sit and do nothing. After describing the needs in western Africa, one leader said wryly, "All it takes is money and people." Why do we think we must kick doors down? They are already wide open.

After a skeptical government official seemed ready to close the door on mission work in the Bahamas, a church representative told her, "If we need to leave the Bahamas, we will. But then we will go and do what good we can somewhere else where we are welcome." At this, the official's attitude changed, and the door to the Bahamas remained open.

Option 3 has some fringe benefits. It relates to option 2! Because we see how other people live, we feel more like conserving resources for their sake. We can even go back to option 1! We might ask government authorities for specific considerations, which is quite different from entering politics and pressuring the government for reforms.

What about the matter of helping people to help themselves? Many have-nots are responsible for their own poverty, right? Right, but that is not true of *every* have-not. In many poor countries, a few rich people or foreign companies own most of the land, and the poor must scratch on the rest of it. Most of the food raised by large landholders (such as bananas, sugar, pineapples, and coffee) is shipped out of the country to people who can afford to buy it. All this is not necessarily the fault of the poor people.

"And what about this man who claims that Christ is the answer? With heart tinged with emotion, he packs his bags and takes the next boat to Africa, to reach the black man with the Gospel. He spends millions of dollars . . . he goes through all kinds of sacrifices; he'll contract malaria; he'll get shot; he'll lose his own children in order to go to the mission field to reach the black man in Africa with the Gospel.

"But he won't cross the street."[8]

While reaching out to the have-nots in other countries, we should also notice the have-nots in our own country and community. People who hope to serve on the foreign field should be busy doing good at home. As one missionary put it, "Don't send the people you can spare. We can spare them here too."

Should missionaries adopt the lifestyle of the poor around them? Not always. Such a move could be looked upon as affectation. But they can at least avoid flaunting wealth, such as by not snapping cameras frequently. A camera costs several months' wages in some countries.

A man was traveling on a train in a foreign country. As night fell and it became cool, he thought of putting on the sweater he had in his suitcase. But he had second thoughts when he noticed the ragged boys around him shivering in the chilly air. In his case, even putting on a sweater might have flaunted his wealth.

Avoiding Accidents With Money

Flip open a typical driver's education textbook, and you will find a chapter titled "The Traffic Accident Problem." In fact, virtually all the chapters in such a book have something to do with preventing accidents. For accidents kill, and everyone knows of someone who has been killed in a traffic accident.

Why? What is the problem?

It is a truism, but nevertheless a truth worth considering: accidents happen by accident. Someone is surprised. What about a man who deliberately drove off a cliff—he was not surprised, was he? No. But then the wreck he had was not an accident either, because he did it on purpose. Face it: accidents happen when people are taken unawares. Police have lost count of the times they have heard drivers say, "I never even saw the other car."

Soul-destroying accidents with money also take place because someone was surprised. Not that he wasn't warned. The Bible contains many warnings about amassing wealth. But still it is easy to say, "I think I can handle this."

In a highway accident, a driver might destroy his car yet survive himself, a sadder but wiser man. That can happen financially too, if someone makes a major financial blunder and learns a good lesson from it. But often it happens the other way around. A man can handle his finances skillfully and still destroy himself.

Rarely does it happen that a driver is killed, while his vehicle gets by without a scratch. But in the world of finances, it happens all the time. There are many, many accidents with money— accidents in which the money survives but the owner is destroyed and never knows what hit him.

> *"Whom the gods would destroy, they first make mad with power."*
> *—Old proverb*

Indeed, one can be destroyed by money he does not even have. "They that *will* [want to] be rich fall into temptation and a snare, and into many foolish and hurtful lusts." And again, "The love of money is the root of all evil: which while some *coveted* after, they have erred from the faith" (1 Timothy 6:9, 10). You can destroy yourself by having an undue desire for money, even if you do not have any money.

The matter of power enters the picture. One-horsepower buggies usually do not collide with trees, walls, or each other (though a runaway horse is not unheard of). But the power of four hundred horses under a hood has ruined many a young man.

What do the authorities do to cut down the number of accidents? Since surprises are a problem, and power creates many of the surprises, they regulate the power. Speed limits illustrate this. So do arrests for not respecting the limits. So do high insurance rates for high-powered cars.

The car manufacturers themselves have helped to change the power mentality. Today they emphasize economy rather than power. Even the speedometers are less likely to show figures like *120 mph* in favor of a more conservative *100* or even *80*.

Wealth too is power. Some people can handle more of it than others, but everyone has his limits. God knows all this and has chosen not to give too much of it to people. He gives some people no choice in the matter. He gives other people the chance to ruin themselves if they choose, but He warns them not to do it.

Most readers of this book come in the class of people who could ruin themselves if they chose to. Once again, it is like driving a car. The power is available. You have to resist the temptation.

Previous chapters spoke more specifically of how to resist that temptation. This chapter merely lays down a principle. Before we move on, we will look at wealth from a different perspective, using a different comparison.

Avoiding Addiction to Money

The rich young ruler was a money addict. The only way Jesus could free him from the clutches of his own wealth was to rid him of it all. You might say, "Fine, I'll have lots of money but just not become addicted to it." And that is

> *"It may get you while you are getting it, and having gotten it, it may have you bound by chains of which you are not aware."*[9]

theoretically possible. But how often does it actually happen? The trouble is the same with money as with drugs. You do not realize you are hooked until you try to get unhooked. Then you realize just how strong the chains of addiction are.

Yes, you can have money without being addicted to it, and you can be addicted to it without having it. We are quick to point this out—a little too quick. Jesus did not emphasize this concept at all. Rather, He emphasized the other side—that if you have it, you are extremely likely to be addicted. Worse, you are extremely likely not even to know it.

Naturally, we wonder if there is a way to have our cake and eat it too. Can we not somehow have wealth—since there is so much of it in this country and it is so easy to get—and still have treasure in heaven?

There is one thing we can do. Suppose you walk down the street to the bank carrying half a million dollars. You can do this with absolutely no danger to your spiritual life on one condition—*if the money is not yours.* It happens all the time. People handle huge sums of money every day and live perfectly normal lives because they know the money belongs to someone else.

> *Limit the amount your children can have, even if you think they can handle it. Most of what they earn at first should go to you as parents.*

Some Christians have caught this concept by seeing saint after saint succumb to his own wealth. They decide they will handle money just as if it were not their own. I do not mean that they merely change their attitude toward money. (Attitude can be pretty hard to define in a case like this!) They *act* right too. They live in humble homes, sit on furniture that shows signs of wear, drive no-name used cars, and put on the same clothes they wore last year. They wear things out. The money in their bank account over and above their simple needs is not for them. It is for giving (or lending at low or no interest) to the work of the church, or maybe to help some struggling young man buy a farm.

An example of such a man was a Frenchman named Guizon, who labored all his life but lived on the simplest of fare. Although he was honest and kind, neighborhood boys seeing him pass by would shout, "There goes old Skinflint!" Guizon was over eighty years old when he died, friendless and despised. But in his will he stated, "I was once poor, and I observed that the people of Marseilles suffered extremely for the want of pure water. Having no family, I have devoted my life to the saving of a sum of money sufficient to build an aqueduct to supply the poor of the city of Marseilles with pure water, so that the poorest may have a full supply." Over his lifetime, he had amassed a fortune in gold and silver worth two hundred thousand dollars.[10]

By now you are saying, "We're back to the same proposition. That isn't *having* wealth; it's just *holding* wealth!" An excellent point. The money we have is ours only to hold, which is another way of saying it is not ours at all. We just think it is.

God's Word makes this point over and over.

- "All the earth is mine" (Exodus 19:5).
- "The land shall not be sold for ever: for the land is mine; for ye are strangers and sojourners with me" (Leviticus 25:23). This was spoken to the Israelites some time before they entered Canaan.
- "For every beast of the forest is mine, and the cattle upon a thousand hills. I know all the fowls of the mountains: and the wild beasts of the field are mine. If I were hungry, I would not tell thee: for the world is mine, and the fulness thereof" (Psalm 50:10–12).
- The silver is mine, and the gold is mine, saith the LORD of hosts" (Haggai 2:8).

- The earth is the LORD's, and the fulness thereof; the world, and they that dwell therein" (Psalm 24:1).
- "Whether we live therefore, or die, we are the Lord's" (Romans 14:8).

Logically, then, we do not have to *act as if* the money is not ours. The money really *is not* ours. We have no more right to dip into it for our personal pleasure than Judas had the right to dip into "the bag" that he carried (John 12:6).

Does this mean we should never again buy a pack of salted peanuts? No, it does not mean we must go through life without enjoying anything. But it might mean reevaluating what we enjoy. Simple pleasures can be more exquisite than elaborate ones. Maybe we should spend more time beholding the fowls of the air or the lilies of the field. After all, isn't that what we intended to do when we bought those field guides to birds and flowers?

This does not mean we should be "sloppy poor" either, if we can help it. John Bunyan had the same concern. He described Christians who presented themselves with "here a rag, and there a rent, to the disparagement of their Lord."[11] Conspicuous poverty has no value in itself.

Neither should all Christians draw the line at exactly the same place. Some think it important to have mattresses that do not sag. Some emphasize well-fitting shoes. Some consider it necessary for their children to have straight teeth. Rather than criticizing what others do or fail to do, we need to evaluate what God wants us to do personally.

Finally, no one can guarantee that by resolving to live a simple lifestyle, any Christian can safely keep a large bank account. That is one reason why Jesus told the rich young ruler, "Sell all." He knew that the young man should not even try to *control* it. And that is one reason why God never lets many of us become well-to-do in the first place. He knows we simply would not be able to handle wealth. He withholds it from us so that He will not lose us.

> *While other passions grow weaker with age, the love of money seems to grow stronger.*

The Puzzling Parable of Luke 16

1. There was a certain rich man, which had a steward; and the same was accused unto him that he had wasted his goods. 2. And he called him, and said unto him, How is it that I hear this of thee? give an account of thy stewardship; for thou mayest be no longer steward. 3. Then the steward said within himself, What shall I do? for my lord taketh away from me the stewardship: I cannot dig; to beg I am ashamed. 4. I am resolved what to do, that, when I am put out of the stewardship, they may receive me into their houses. 5. So he called every one of his lord's debtors unto him, and said unto the first, How much owest thou unto my lord? 6. And he said, An hundred measures of oil. And he said unto him, Take thy bill, and sit down quickly, and write fifty. 7. Then said he to another, And how much owest thou? And he said, An hundred measures of wheat. And he said unto him, Take thy bill, and write fourscore. 8. And the lord commended the unjust steward, because he had done wisely: for the children of this world are in their generation wiser than the children of light. 9. And I say unto you, Make to yourselves friends of the mammon of unrighteousness; that, when ye fail, they may receive you into everlasting habitations.

Bible students still puzzle over the story that Jesus told in Luke 16. With all respect to various interpretations of this parable, here is one interpretation and a few observations.

It seems that the steward was an unprincipled man. He was being fired for wasting his master's goods, so it is a fair guess that he had in fact wasted them. But he was a shrewd man. He still had a bit of time to manage his master's goods before he had to head out the door. So he gave his master's customers a rebate on some goods they had bought.

It is not clear whether he had the authority to do this. Perhaps he was cheating his master by so doing. On the other hand, perhaps he was granting the rebate out of a markup he had been planning to put into his own pocket. At any rate, he needed generous friends in a hurry, and he thought that being generous was a good way to make them. It was a shabby scheme; but from the steward's point of view, it was better than nothing.

Afterward his employer discovered what he had done and gave him his grudging admiration. The steward had "done wisely"— well, at least shrewdly. He had shown foresight. He had recognized that "a friend in need is a friend indeed," and he acted to make friends indeed.

Our Lord commented, "The children of this world are in their generation wiser than the children of light." In other words, this steward acted more wisely in his sphere than God's children often act in theirs. The children of light don't proceed as logically from their assumptions as the children of the world do. Jesus threw out the challenge: If this is what you believe, why don't you act as if you believe it?

"And I say unto you, Make to yourselves friends [with] the mammon of unrighteousness [it is "filthy lucre," but we can use it to make friends]; that, when ye fail, they may receive you into everlasting habitations." These friends could be angels, departed saints—yes, God Himself. What could "everlasting habitations" be but heaven? By the way we handle money, we can make friends— friends eager to greet us when our bodies fail here and we enter the gates of glory.

Although Jesus did not mention it here, making such friends has more than a future benefit. It has a present benefit. With God Himself for a present friend, imagine the security. Jesus used the expression "when ye fail" to refer to the

> *Money in the bank makes money. Money in the offering makes friends, here and in the world to come.*

point of death. But we fail in little ways between here and there. If God is equal to our final physical bankruptcy (death), is He not equal to our present fiascos? Of course He is. And there lies a great deal of security.

Conclusion

In 586 B.C., the thing Jerusalem greatly feared came to pass. Her starving warriors could no longer defend the city walls, and sturdy enemy soldiers pushed their way in. They "had no compassion upon young man or maiden, old man, or him that stooped for age" (2 Chronicles 36:17). The king of Jerusalem fled but was caught. The enemy slew his sons before his very eyes, then gouged out his eyes and took him and thousands of other captives to Babylon.

All this should have come as no surprise. The "weeping prophet" Jeremiah had warned his people over and over that unless they repented, they could expect only disaster. And now it had come.

Was there no hope for restoration? Oh, yes, there was hope. The Jews would return to their homeland. But they would have to wait for seventy years—an impossibly long time for anyone already in middle age, and depressingly long even for the young.

But why seventy? Why not a nice round figure of fifty, or better yet, twenty, or even ten? Because God's law of retribution worked that way. Seventy years of captivity paid in misery for seventy offenses.

And what were the seventy offenses? Here is the interesting thing. Not seventy murders, not seventy scandals in royal families, not seventy idols, not seventy abominations. Rather, God counted seventy years because of the years in which the Israelites had failed to heed an old law. God had instructed them to let the land rest every seven years, not even harvesting the volunteer crops but leaving them for the poor. They had failed to do this. (Compare 2 Chronicles 36:21 with Exodus 23:10, 11).

Seventy years of captivity for a pocketbook issue! And a nitpicker's issue at that—as many Israelites probably thought. To them, it must have seemed totally unrealistic to let the land lie fallow for a whole year once every seven years. So the matter was quietly dropped. After all (many a man must have reasoned), no one else was doing it either. If anyone had dared to mention it, others might have said, "God means well, but we have to be realistic about such matters."

For seventy times seven years, God said little about this, but He had the last word in the end. The land had seventy years to rest, and Israel had seventy years to think. Economics had made all the difference.

But we need not close on such a negative note. Life moved on, even for the Israelite captives. Not even Babylon turned out to be a complete dead end for them. "Build ye houses, and dwell in them; and plant gardens, and eat the fruit of them," they had been told (Jeremiah 29:5). They would be given another chance, even if a limited one, to practice good economics.

And so it is for us. Even if we are paying dearly for our mistakes, the end of the road is not yet, nor will we find ourselves at a complete dead end as long as we live. There is a pathway leading to God from any spot where we may stand. Life is still a journey. May God bless you, fellow traveler.

> Sign in front of a church:
> "If you are on the wrong road,
> God allows U-turns."

Notes

Chapter One: Planning

[1] Source unknown.

[2] *Reader's Digest,* April 1999, p. 138.

[3] Anonymous, *The Christian Contender,* January 1993, p. 6.

[4] English proverb.

[5] Robert J. Morgan, *Nelson's Complete Book of Stories, Illustrations, and Quotes* (Nashville: Thomas Nelson Publishers, c. 2000), p. 575.

[6] George Müller, *The Autobiography of George Müller,* ed. Diana L. Matisko (Springdale, Pa.: Whitaker House, 1984), p. 220.

Chapter Two: Earning

[1] *American Heritage Dictionary*

[2] Peter T. White, "The Power of Money," *National Geographic,* January 1993, p. 84.

[3] Author compared U.S. and world populations (1 to 24) along with the fact that the U.S. produces about 1/5 of the world's gross product. *1998 Time Almanac, p.175.*

[4] Robert Eby, "Maintaining Good Works for Necessary Uses," *The Eastern Mennonite Testimony,* (September 1997), p. 6.

[5] Denis Haack, *The Rest of Success* (Downers Grove, Ill.: InterVarsity Press, 1989), p. 114.

[6] Said of Sinclair Lewis. Quoted in *Ten Best Books* (New York: The Reader's Digest Association Incorporated, 1964), p. 1.

[7] Russell H. Conwell, *Acres of Diamonds* (Westwood, N.J.: Fleming H. Revell Co., 1960), pp. 32, 33.

[8] Fred Lumb, *What Every Woman Should Know About Finances* (Rockville Centre, N.Y.: Farnsworth Publishing Company, 1978), p. 191.

[9] David Stewart, *Network Marketing Action Guide* (Scottsdale, Ariz.: Success in Action, 1991), p. 37.

[10] Raymond M. Weaver, "Financial Solvency," *The Eastern Mennonite Testimony,* January 1988, p. 8.

[11] Weaver, *Testimony,* p. 7.

[12] A. I. Root, *ABC and XYZ of Beekeeping* (Medina, Ohio: A. I. Root Co., 1966), p. 476.

[13] Howard Landis, "To Those Who Might Become Farmers," *The Gospel Herald,* August 20, 1985, p. 577.

[14] Simeon Rudolph, "Single-income Households," *Home Horizons,* March 2005, p. 2.

Chapter Three: Economizing

[1] Leon Sensenig, " 'What Shall We Do for the Hundred Talents?' " *The Eastern Mennonite Testimony,* August 1988, pp. 8, 9.

[2] Glenn M. Sensenig, "The Look of Luxury," *The Eastern Mennonite Testimony,* July 1987, p. 16.

[3] Joanne Coughran, *Victory at the Super-Market* (Wheaton, Ill.: Tyndale House Publishers, Inc., 1984), p. 21.

[4] Ibid., p. 35, 36.

[5] David Wagler, "The BIGGEST Waste in the World," *Family Life,* February 1974.

[6] Coughran, *Super-Market,* p. 38.

[7] Robert T. Kiyosaki and Sharon L. Lechter, *Rich Dad, Poor Dad* (New York: Warner Books, 1997, 1998) p. 89.

[8] Jonathan D. Pond, *1001 Ways to Cut Your Expenses* (New York: Dell Publishing, 1992), p. 103.

[9] Ron Blue, *Sneakers From Heaven* (Anaheim, Cal.: Insight for Living, 1991), p. 92.

[10] Source unknown.

[11] Fred V. Hein and Dana L. Farnsworth, *Living* (Glenview, Ill.: Scott, Foresman and Company, 1965), p. 32.

[12] Scottish proverb, quoted in Norman V. Hope, "Being Christian in an Affluent Society," *Christianity Today,* February 14, 1969, p. 7.

[13] John Alexander, quoted in Doris Janzen Longacre, *Living More With Less* (Scottdale, Pa.: Herald Press, 1980), p. 171.

[14] Source unknown.

[15] Morgan, *Stories,* p. 420.

[16] Original story by Homer J. Livingstone, Chicago bank president, quoted in *Fortune,* cited in Hillel Black, *Buy Now, Pay Later* (New York: Pocket Books, Inc., 1961), p. 106.

[17] Rudyard Kipling, in the poem "If."

[18] Melvin S. Burkholder, "The Insurance Bondage," *The Eastern Mennonite Testimony,* February 1991, p. 8.

[19] Ibid., p. 8.

[20] Barbara Keener Shank, *Rimes for Our Times* (Lancaster, Pa.: Barkeesh Enterprises, 1979), p. 15.

[21] Glen E. Auker, "Life Insurance—When the Mennonites Said NO," *The Eastern Mennonite Testimony,* February 1992, p. 5.

[22] Ron Blue, *Master Your Money* (Nashville: Thomas Nelson Publishers, 1986), p. 214.

[23] David Chilton, *The Wealthy Barber* (Toronto: Stoddart Publishing Co., 1989), p. 176.

[24] Quoted in Grant Jeffrey, *Final Warning* (Toronto: Frontier Research Publications, 1995), p. 283.

[25] "Newslines," *The Sword and Trumpet,* July 1987, p. 12.

[26] Charles Long, *How to Survive Without a Salary* (Toronto: Warwick Publishing Co., 1996), p. 181.

[27] Kiyosaki, *Dad,* p. 104.

[28] Lumb, *Finances,* p.198.

[29] *World Book,* articles "Euthanasia" and "Death."

[30] *World Book,* article "Living Will."

[31] *World Book,* article "Euthanasia."

[32] Doug Podolsky, "A Right-to-die Reminder," *US News & World Report,* December 2, 1991, p. 74.

[33] George R. Brunk II, "Is Cremation for Christians?" *The Sword and Trumpet,* July 1991.

Chapter Four: Investing

[1] Attributed to Mark Twain.

[2] Martin Luther, quoted in Morgan, *Stories,* p. 333.

[3] Alexander McKenzie, *Getting One's Bearings* (New York: Fleming H. Revell Co., 1903), p. 133.

[4] Ibid., p. 195.

[5] *Encarta Encyclopedia,* article "Corporate Finance."

[6] "Dollar in the Doldrums," *Youth News,* Date unknown, p. 1.

[7] *Encarta Encyclopedia,* article "Stocks."

[8] Ravi Batra, *Surviving the Great Depression of 1990* (New York: Dell Publishing Co., Inc., 1988), pp. 161, 162.

[9] Ibid., p. 167.

[10] Ibid., p. 169.

[11] Jeffrey, *Warning,* p. 240.

[12] Ibid., p. 244.

[13] David A. Fisher, *World History for Christian Schools,* (Greenville, S.C.: Bob Jones University Press, 1984), p. 561.

[14] Chilton, *Barber,* p. 167.

[15] Kiyosaki, *Dad,* p. 73.

[16] Shakespeare, *Hamlet,* 1.3, cited in Lumb, *Finances,* p. 115.

[17] Wayne Wenger, "The Application of Usury," *The Christian Contender,* October 1989, p. 10.

[18] Wesley A. Petre, "Money—Its Implications," *The Christian Contender,* September 2001, p. 11.

[19] *World Book,* article "Trust Fund."

[20] Frances Johnson Roberts, "The Bank of Heaven" (Warrenton, Mo.: Child Evangelism Fellowship, 1975).

[21] Kenneth Taylor and Virginia Muir, *My Life: A Guided Tour* (Wheaton, Ill.: Tyndale House Publishers, 1991), p. 196.

[22] Watchman Nee, *The Normal Christian Life* (Wheaton, Ill.: Tyndale House Publishers, 1957), p. 270.

[23] Paul White, *Alias Jungle Doctor* (Exeter, Devon, England: Paternoster Press Ltd., 1977), p. 220.

[24] *World Book,* article "Social Security."

[25] Raymond Zook, "The Sweeping Tide of Materialism," *The Christian Contender,* July 1995, p. 7.

[26] *World Book,* article "Pension."

[27] Batra, *Depression,* p. 203.

[29] *World Book,* article "Pension."

[29] Batra, *Depression,* p. 203.

[30] Larry Burkett, *The Coming Economic Earthquake* (Chicago: Moody Press, 1994), p. 139.

Chapter Five: Borrowing

[1] Quoted in Edwin G. West and Roger LeRoy Miller, *Canadian Economics Today: The Macro View* (New York: Harper & Row, 1978), p. 216.

[2] Wesley A. Petre, "Money—Its Implications," *The Christian Contender,* September 2001, p. 10.

[3] Fred Nighswander, "Frugality," *The Christian Contender,* May 1987, p. 12.

[4] Müller, *Autobiography,* p. 214.

[5] Sign on an IBM executive's office, quoted in George and Marjean Fooshee, *You Can Beat the Money Squeeze* (Old Tappan, N.J.: Fleming H. Revell Company, 1980), p. 18.

[6] Ibid., pp. 58, 59.

[7] Jeffrey, *Warning,* p. 279.

[8] Ibid., p. 279.

[9] Chilton, *Barber,* p. 135.

[10] Blue, *Sneakers,* p. 13.

[11] Dave Ramsey, *Financial Peace* (New York: Penguin Books, 1997), p. 266.

[12] Müller, *Autobiography,* pp. 161, 162.

Chapter Six: Giving

[1] Katie Funk Wiebe, "Getting Into the Pit," *Gospel Herald,* January 8, 1985, p. 19.

[2] A caption to a picture of two children sleeping in the street. Quoted in Brenda Stoltzfus, "What to Do Wth Beggars?" *Gospel Herald,* June 11, 1985, p. 410.

[3] Frances R. Havergal, *Kept for the Master's Use* (Chicago: Homewood Publishing Company, 1879), p. 101.

[4] Andrew Murray, *Money* (Minneapolis, Minn.: Bethany Fellowship, Inc., 1978), pp. 12, 13.

[5] R. G. LeTourneau, *Mover of Men and Mountains* (Chicago: Moody Press, 1967), pp. 173, 189.

[6] Scott Burns, "A Surprising Portrait of Charity in America," *Dallas Morning News,* November 25, 1986, p. 1. Cited in Batra, *Depression,* p. 241.

[7] Reginald H. Roy, *David Lam: A Biography* (Vancouver: Douglas & McIntyre Ltd., 1996), pp. 189, 190. Reprinted with permission from the publisher.

[8] Julius Segal, *Winning Life's Toughest Battles* (New York: Ivy Books, 1986), p. 105, cited in Morgan, *Stories,* pp. 340, 341.

[9] Coughran, *Super-Market,* p. 279.

[10] Murray, *Money,* p. 45.

[11] David W. Shank, *Mennonite Safari* (Scottdale, Pa.: Herald Press, 1974), p. 128.

[12] James Baer, "Keeping Brotherhood Aid Alive," *The Christian Contender,* June 1999, p. 2.

Chapter Seven: Thinking Out Loud

[1] *Youth News,* Date unknown.

[2] George Klippenstein, "The Mark," *The Christian Contender,* June 1998, p. 11.

[3] *"Others May . . . You Cannot,"* (Grand Rapids: Faith, Prayer, and Tract League.)

[4] Attributed to Helen Keller.

[5] Longacre, *Living,* p. 26.

[6] Stanley Wine, "Extravagance and Waste," *The Eastern Mennonite Testimony,* May 1991, p. 16.

[7] Stephen J. Champ, "Scriptural Concepts of Economics," *The Christian School Builder,* December 2005, p. 105.

[8] Tom Skinner, *Black and Free* (Grand Rapids: Zondervan Publishing House, 1968), p. 31.

[9] A. Mennonite Poorman, "So You Have Money," *The Sword and Trumpet,* Fourth Quarter 1952, p. 13.

[10] Anonymous, "The Sacrifice of a Frenchman," *The Christian Contender,* September 1987, p. 15.

[11] John Bunyan, *Pilgrim's Progress,* Part 2. This statement was made by Mr. Dare-Not-Lie in Vanity Fair.

Scripture Index

Index